Web Portals and
Higher Education

Richard N. Katz and Associates

Web Portals and Higher Education

Technologies to Make IT Personal

A Joint Publication of EDUCAUSE and NACUBO
Sponsored by Oracle Corporation and KPMG Consulting

JOSSEY-BASS
A Wiley Company
San Francisco

Published by

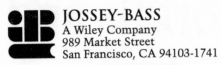

JOSSEY-BASS
A Wiley Company
989 Market Street
San Francisco, CA 94103-1741

www.josseybass.com

Jossey-Bass books and products are available through most bookstores. To contact Jossey-Bass directly, call (888) 378-2537, fax to (800) 605-2665, or visit our website at www.josseybass.com.

Substantial discounts on bulk quantities of Jossey-Bass books are available to corporations, professional associations, and other organizations. For details and discount information, contact the special sales department at Jossey-Bass.

We at Jossey-Bass strive to use the most environmentally sensitive paper stocks available to us. Our publications are printed on acid-free recycled stock whenever possible, and our paper always meets or exceeds minimum GPO and EPA requirements.

Library of Congress Cataloging-in-Publication Data

Web portals and higher education: Technologies to make IT personal/
Richard N. Katz, editor.—1st ed.
    p. cm. — (The Jossey-Bass higher and adult education series)
Includes bibliographical references and index.
    ISBN 0-7879-6171-X (alk. paper)
    1. Internet in higher education.   2. Educational technology.
3. Information technology.   I. Katz, Richard N.   II. Series.
    LB1044.87 .P73   2002
    378.1'7344678—dc21   2001007668

FIRST EDITION
PB Printing   10 9 8 7 6 5 4 3 2 1

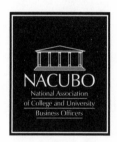

EDUCAUSE advances higher education by promoting the intelligent use of information technology through professional development activities, publications, policy and research initiatives, recognition programs, and online information services. The EDUCAUSE membership comprises more than 1,800 colleges, universities, education organizations, and corporations. Information about membership, programs, and services is available at www.educause.edu.

KPMG Consulting Over twenty years ago, KPMG Consulting, Inc. became one of the first major companies to designate a specific vertical practice to provide technology and management consulting services for higher education. Today, KPMG is the leading service provider in this arena, with dedicated consultants who offer deep technology and industry expertise. KPMG serves over fifty colleges and universities, including George Washington University, Yale University, and Stanford University.

The National Association of College and University Business Officers (NACUBO) is the preeminent association for those involved in the leadership, management, and administration of higher education. NACUBO members are the chief administrative and financial officers at more than 2,100 colleges and universities. For more information, go to www.nacubo.org.

ORACLE Oracle Higher Education is the world's leading supplier of software for information management for higher education institutions globally. The company develops and distributes software that helps institutions manage and grow their businesses. In addition to computer software products, Oracle Higher Education offers its customers a range of consulting, education, and support services.

Contents

Foreword

Once again, campuses are considering an opportunity to move to a new level of service effectiveness through the application of technology. In the current instance, the technology at issue is the portal and the opportunities it creates for the enhanced use of e-business. Based on the information exchanged at two forums organized by EDUCAUSE and NACUBO, portals and a set of related technologies are raising nearly as many questions as the number of answers they provide. As discussed in this volume, however, answers exist, and it behooves chief business officers and chief information officers to work together to make the best strategic decisions for their specific situation.

There is ample evidence to suggest that many aspects of higher education are being transformed through an e-revolution. One year ago the portal was considered to be at the core of this revolution, bringing with it a need for new business models.[1] These models will entail opportunities for campuses to make major investments independently, in partnership with vendors, or through collaborations among institutions. Increasingly, portals are understood to be an important layer in an overall institutional information technology (IT) architecture—a layer that provides a means to integrate information and services consumed or created by the campus community.

As with so many information technologies and change strategies, there is no one-size-fits-all approach. In fact, there may be as many approaches to portals as colors in the rainbow. Some of the approaches will prove to be poor investments, possibly with vendors who will not survive the initial contract period. For others, careful choices will result in significant competitive advantages relative to their peer institutions.

Once a college or university decides to enter this brave new world, a variety of decisions need to be made, including those as basic as whether to buy, build, or partner to acquire the technology. There is no shortage of firms competing to be the vendor of choice for higher education portals and e-business solutions. Nonetheless, in the one-year period between the two events that refined this content, many firms have entered this arena, have gone out of business, or have been acquired under distressed circumstances. In some cases, vendors have restructured their product architectures to exploit the power of the Internet more fully and to better integrate the portal with Web, security, customer relationship management (CRM), and enterprise resource management (ERP) layers and applications.

In this same time period, a consortium of colleges and universities has worked to support the release of uPortal, a technical framework for assembling and organizing college and university content and service "channels."

Rather than working with a vendor, campuses may decide that it's more effective to acquire the tools and other resources needed to develop an in-house solution. This should result in enhanced control over the ultimate solution, but there is no guarantee that it will prove to be cost-effective over the long term. Given the dynamic environment of the technology and the difficulty in retaining staff, the developers may have moved on when it comes time to upgrade to the next level.

A third approach—partnering—might be the most effective for some. There are multiple ways to approach a partnership, including working in a joint venture with a single vendor or participating in a consortium involving multiple campuses. There are advantages to both approaches and to the many other types of partnerships that could be established to develop portals and engage in e-business activities.

Regardless of the particular approach selected, the most effective applications of portal technology will occur at institutions that consider all campus perspectives. We believe the most successful institutions will be those where the chief business officer (CBO) and the chief information officer (CIO) work in tandem to lead an effort to balance the campus's business, technological, and service perspectives toward achieving its goals. Portals and e-business will serve all facets of the campus, from admissions and athletics to the various academic units and the bookstore. Despite the competing interests and priorities of these diverse units, they must come together under the leadership of the CBO and CIO to ensure that a common approach is taken to gain the most from the technology and the opportunities presented by it.

The chapters in this volume cover a full range of issues to be considered as a result of the new technology and the evolving Internet business environment. The writers examine the business challenges, organizational implications, policy choices, and the technology itself. Many questions are identified, and several solutions are offered. It should be recognized, however, that the environment is far from mature. False starts and other mistakes will be made. We hope the information in this volume will minimize the likelihood of these missteps occurring and the cost of them when they do.

We wish to thank the sponsors of these forums: HigherMarkets, IBM, KPMG Consulting, Oracle, PeopleSoft, and PricewaterhouseCoopers. Special thanks go to Oracle Corporation and KPMG Consulting, whose additional support has made this publication possible. In addition to providing essential financial support for this undertaking, these firms' representatives contributed significantly to the quality of the outcomes through their facilitation during the forum.

Brian L. Hawkins
Jay Morley

Note

1. See especially, *UC 2010: A New Business Architecture for the University of California*. Oakland: University of California, 2000.

Acknowledgments

Acknowledgments are hard to write. More people have a hand in the creation of a book than any reader can imagine, or any author can responsibly thank. Nevertheless, this is a tradition-bound activity and there are indeed people to thank. First and foremost, the literature assembled between these covers emerges from three days of intensive discussion among one of the most gifted groups of higher education executives I have had the honor of working with. Nearly a hundred senior executives are responsible for generating and honing the ideas expressed in this volume. Of course, the delicate polishing of each chapter is the result of the work of the contributing authors. It is not possible to thank them enough.

The forums and this publication have depended on a unique and important partnership between EDUCAUSE and the National Association of College and University Business Officers (NACUBO). The realization of a new technology-enabled vision of higher education depends on the partnership of these organizations. Many members of the staff of EDUCAUSE and NACUBO deserve thanks. Greg Dobbin, Larry Goldstein, Brian Hawkins, Susan Jurow, Jay Morley, Diana Oblinger, and Maryann Terrana deserve special thanks. Of course, this publication would not have achieved liftoff without the financial and intellectual support of Lee Ramsayer and Joan Leonard of Oracle Corporation and the fine higher education team at KPMG

Consulting. The forums themselves depended on the additional support and involvement of PeopleSoft's Susan Beidler, PricewaterhouseCooper's Jill Kidwell, IBM's Mike King, and HigherMarket's Paul Salsgiver.

Most successful projects benefit from lots of advice, both formal and informal. This one is no different. On the formal level, the EDUCAUSE Advisory Group on Administrative Information Systems and Services has consistently risen above its calling to design the forums that have generated this volume. In addition, a small group of people has worked quietly over the last year to enhance one another's understanding of these complex issues. I owe a great intellectual debt of gratitude to Jim Dolgonas, Weldon Ihrig, Robert Kvavik, Ed Lightfoot, and Steve Relyea.

There are editors and there are editors. I have had the great pleasure of working with Karen Bandy of Akilah Media on this project. Karen is a wonderful colleague who provided gently balanced encouragement, sympathy, and discipline throughout this project. Gale Erlandson was my editor at Jossey-Bass for four years. Together we forged an important relationship between EDUCAUSE and Jossey-Bass. She recently left this fine publishing organization and I will miss her. David Brightman and his team have stepped into the fray and continue to provide great editorial leadership and support.

Last, only because I am a private person, I'd like to thank my wife, Peggy Rogers, and my son, Anthony Clyde. Their love, patience, and understanding of my quirky nature make it possible for me to pursue this somewhat solitary endeavor within a broader context of belonging.

Richard N. Katz
Boulder, Colorado

Forum Participants, 2001–2002

Steve Barclay, University of California, San Francisco
Greg J. Baroni, formerly with KPMG Consulting, Inc.
Susan Beidler, PeopleSoft, Inc.
Wendell C. Brase, University of California, Irvine
Lauren J. Brisky, Vanderbilt University
Neal M. Callander, NACUBO
Charles J. Carter, Western Carolina University
J. Reid Christenberry, Georgia State University
Arnold B. Combe, University of Utah
Larry D. Conrad, Florida State University
Ruth Constantine, Smith College
John R. Curry, Massachusetts Institute of Technology
D. Teddy Diggs, EDUCAUSE
Jim Dolgonas, University of California, Office of the President
Phillip L. Doolittle, University of Redlands
William R. Durgin, College of the Holy Cross
Jack Duwe, University of Wisconsin-Madison
David J. Ernst, California State University, Office of the Chancellor
Jennifer L. Foutty, Indiana University
Paul B. Gandel, University of Rhode Island
Rufus Glasper, Maricopa Community College District
Bernard W. Gleason, Boston College
Cynthia Golden, Duquesne University

Larry Goldstein, Campus Strategies
Lev S. Gonick, California State University-Monterey Bay
Rhonda I. Gross, Case Western Reserve University
Elazar C. Harel, University of California, San Diego
Mernoy E. Harrison, Arizona State University
James R. Henderson, Florida State University
Susan Hoffman, Vanderbilt University
Darrel S. Huish, Arizona State University
Carl W. Jacobson, University of Delaware
Susan Jurow, NACUBO
Richard N. Katz, EDUCAUSE
Jillinda J. Kidwell, PricewaterhouseCoopers LLP
Michael D. King, IBM Corporation
Donna Klinger, NACUBO
Paul J. Kobulnicky, University of Connecticut
David W. Koehler, Princeton University
Robert B. Kvavik, University of Minnesota
Lucinda Lea, Middle Tennessee State University
Edward Lightfoot, University of Washington
Robert L. Lovitt, University of Texas at Dallas
Scott Ludlow, Clemson University
Mark A. Luker, EDUCAUSE
Polley Ann McClure, Cornell University
William A. McCune, West Virginia University
Patrick McElroy, Learning Content Exchange, Inc.
Marilyn A. McMillan, New York University
Barbara H. Morgan, University of California, Berkeley
Sherri L. Newcomb, California State University-Fullerton
Colleen Nickles, California State University-Monterey Bay
Diana G. Oblinger, EDUCAUSE Center for Applied Research
John Palmucci, Loyola College in Maryland
Roger Patterson, University of North Carolina at Chapel Hill
Margaret Pickett, Iowa State University

Margaret F. Plympton, Lehigh University
Lee Ramsayer, Oracle Corporation
Steven W. Relyea, University of California, San Diego
Jenny Rickard, PeopleSoft, Inc.
Julia A. Rudy, EDUCAUSE
James Ryan, The Pennsylvania State University
Paul Salsgiver, HigherMarkets
John R. Schroeder, Maricopa Community College District
Donald Z. Spicer, University System of Maryland
Karin Steinbrenner, University of North Carolina at Charlotte
Mary E. Stephens, California State University-Stanislaus
Howard Strauss, Princeton University
Candace Lerner Street, NACUBO
Ann E. Stunden, University of Wisconsin-Madison
David G. Swartz, The George Washington University
M. Lewis Temares, University of Miami
Maryann Terrana, NACUBO
Terri-Lynn B. Thayer, Brown University
Jane W. Thompson, University of Pittsburgh
David L. Tomcheck, University of California, Irvine
Amelia A. Tynan, University of Rochester
Daniel A. Updegrove, University of Texas at Austin
Jeff von Munkwitz-Smith, University of Connecticut
Patricia M. Wallace, University of Maryland
John F. Walsh, Indiana University
Robert P. Weir, Northeastern University
Kay Whyburn, Texas Tech University

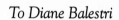

To Diane Balestri

The Authors

Greg Anderson is a student solutions pre-sales consultant in the higher education division of the Oracle Corporation. He has over eleven years of professional experience working within higher education in the areas of student affairs and academic affairs. Anderson specializes in customer relationship management (CRM), the Oracle Student System, student affairs administration, and organizational leadership and change.

Patricia M. Cuocco is the senior director for technology advice and policy at the California State University (CSU) Office of the Chancellor. She has been involved with almost every major technology initiative at CSU for the last sixteen years. Cuocco has a B.A. in English from CSU, Los Angeles, and an M.A. in public policy and administration from CSU, Long Beach.

John R. Curry is the executive vice president of Massachusetts Institute of Technology (MIT) and is responsible for the overall leadership, management, and organization of the institute's administrative and financial affairs. From 1995 to 1998, he served as vice president for business and finance for the California Institute of Technology. From 1993 to 1995, Curry held a similar position at the University of California Los Angeles (UCLA). From 1976 to 1993, he served the University of Southern California (USC) in several administrative roles, including the position of vice president for budget and planning.

Stephen L. Daigle is a senior policy associate with the Information Technology Services Division of the California State University Chancellor's Office. He conducts research studies on technology-related issues to inform systemwide planning and policymaking. His doctorate is from Indiana University, and he has worked in academic and technology administration for twenty-five years.

Bernard Gleason is the associate vice president for Information Technology at Boston College. In 1995, Gleason led Boston College's implementation of Project Agora, one of the most comprehensive initiatives to bring innovative voice, video, and computing technologies and Web services to all students, faculty members, and staff members. He has served in a number of leadership roles with CAUSE, EDUCAUSE, NACUBO, and other national organizations and is a past winner of the CAUSE ELITE Award, that organization's highest recognition for leadership.

Larry Goldstein is founder and president of Campus Strategies. Prior to founding Campus Strategies, Goldstein was senior vice president of the National Association of College and University Business Officers (NACUBO), where he directed the Center for Accounting, Finance, and Institutional Management, NACUBO's primary research and product development unit. Goldstein is a certified public accountant and earned his bachelor of accountancy degree at Walsh College (Michigan) and his M.A. in accounting at the University of Virginia.

Gary Grant is the managing director in charge of customer relationship management (CRM) in higher education markets for KPMG Consulting LLC. He has over twenty years of experience providing technology solutions to public sector clients and frequently lectures on technology-related issues. Grant was awarded a B.A. from the University of Kentucky and earned his M.B.A. from George Washington University.

Rhonda I. Gross is senior vice president for finance and administration at Case Western Reserve University. Prior to joining Case Western Reserve, she was vice president for finance and administration at Lehigh University for six years and was employed at the University of Pittsburgh for twenty years in a variety of positions. She began her career in public accounting. Gross is a graduate of Washington University in St. Louis and earned an M.B.A. from Northwestern University. She is a member of the American Institute of Public Accountants.

Brian L. Hawkins is currently president of EDUCAUSE, a professional association of more than eighteen hundred colleges and universities, dedicated to advancing higher education by promoting the intelligent use of information technology. Prior to this position, Hawkins was senior vice president for academic planning and administrative affairs at Brown University.

Weldon Ihrig is executive vice president of the University of Washington, and is responsible for management of all financial and administrative services of the University. He is one of the primary policymakers of the university as a whole and represents the university in political, business, and civic affairs. Ihrig has held executive positions in higher education at Ohio State University and within the Oregon University System. He holds a B.A. in electrical engineering and an M.B.A., both from Ohio State University.

Richard N. Katz has been vice president of EDUCAUSE since 1996 and directs the EDUCAUSE Center for Applied Research. Before joining EDUCAUSE, Katz served the University of California for fourteen years in a variety of management and executive roles. He is the author or editor of more than three dozen books, monographs, and articles on organizational change and information technology in higher education. Mr. Katz holds a B.A. from the University of Pittsburgh and an M.B.A. from UCLA.

Robert B. Kvavik is professor of political science and associate vice president and vice provost at the University of Minnesota. He is the project director of the university's $60 million Enterprise Project to install new computer and software systems for student services, human resources, Web-based systems, and infrastructure, including business process redesign through the use of technology (for example, portals and other Web applications) and e-business applications. Kvavik holds a doctorate from Stanford University.

Edward Lightfoot is director of information systems at the University of Washington, and is responsible for planning, developing, consulting, and supporting university-wide information systems. He has been involved in software and information systems planning, development, and management since 1964—in projects ranging from COBOL compiler development to medical center information systems. Lightfoot holds a B.S. in industrial management from the Georgia Institute of Technology.

James E. (Jay) Morley Jr. served as a senior financial executive on four campuses for twenty-three years. He last served as senior vice president of Cornell University, prior to assuming the presidency of the National Association of College and University Business Officers (NACUBO) in 1995.

Diana Oblinger is currently a senior fellow of the EDUCAUSE Center for Applied Research (ECAR) and is professor of the practice at the Kenan-Flagler School of Business at the University of North Carolina at Chapel Hill. Previously, she was a vice president and chief information officer within the University of North Carolina system. Oblinger also served in a variety of senior positions at IBM Corporation. She is the author or editor of several books and numerous articles on the incorporation of information technologies into higher education.

Howard Strauss is the manager of Academic Applications, a newly formed group at Princeton University that focuses on improving the teaching and research for Princeton faculty members. Previously, Strauss was the manager of Advanced Applications, an advanced technology group that was charged with turning the latest information technology into practical applications. A graduate of Drexel University and Carnegie Mellon University, Strauss is a member of Pearson's Online Learning Advisory Board and is a frequent presenter and contributor to EDUCAUSE and NACUBO.

Web Portals and
Higher Education

It's a Bird! It's a Plane! It's a . . . Portal?

Richard N. Katz

Information technologists yearn to be wordsmiths or pundits. We are at the very least fascinated by language. On the one hand, we are a professional community that has managed to reduce irreducible concepts to streams of incomprehensible acronyms. On the other hand, we borrow rich and descriptive language from other disciplines to illuminate our own. Such terms as *architecture, ecology,* and *webs* have originated elsewhere and emerged anew from the information technology (IT) cauldron, often to reemerge as a new part of the vernacular.

The most recent linguistic borrowing is the term *portal,* which *Winston Dictionary* defines as "a gate, door, or entrance; especially one that is stately and imposing, as of a cathedral." Given the ecclesiastical origins of the modern university, perhaps it is fitting and appropriate that the latest information technology metaphor is one that fits the collegiate idea so well. The term *portal,* however, is a somewhat troublesome metaphor because it leaves as much unanswered as it purports to answer. One might legitimately ask, a doorway to what? What on earth, our campus colleagues must wonder, is a portal strategy, and why is one important to me?

From its invention less than a decade ago, the World Wide Web has purported to be a newsletter, an advertisement, a policy manual, a community gathering spot, a marketplace, a library, and a virtual university. In essence, the Web has elements of all of these things and yet is not any of these things. The Web is the first ever medium that allows essentially anyone to become a content creator, developer, organizer, distributor, broadcaster, intermediary, buyer, or seller at any time (and in fact to be all of these things at different times). As a result, the Web remains today the ultimate frontier. As such, the Web defies precise description or characterization. It is bounded less by physics than by our imaginations; hence our tendency to borrow metaphors.

Frontiers seem to me to be inherently messy places—untidy and even unsafe places that attract adventurers and miscreants and await some measure of guidance, if not law and order. The portal, in this context, is more than a gateway. It is perhaps a unifying principle that may enable organizations—including colleges and universities—to leverage their investments in enterprise systems, in data warehouses, in reengineered institutional processes, and in staff talent.

The Commercial Sector Is Driving the Portal Dialog—for Now

Recognizing the powerful opportunities for colleges and universities to rethink how their Web sites can be reorganized to serve and transform their institutional mission, private firms have been quick to act. Firms such as YouthStream Media, MyBytes, Jenzabar.com, and Campus Pipeline are offering colleges and universities sophisticated Web sites through which students can obtain campus (and other) information and engage various institutional services. Other firms, such as Click2learn.com, Hungry Minds, Blackboard, and Ziff Davis, are seeking to attract students to specialized learning portals.

Many campuses have also been quick to recognize the powerful and transformational potential of portals and have developed and implemented their own. Many of our colleagues from institutions such as Louisiana State University, Buffalo University, University of British Columbia, and the University of Washington presented their experiences in this arena at EDUCAUSE conferences in 2000 and 2001.

Finally, some of the technologies underlying the Web—Java, in particular—are making it possible for colleges and universities to develop shareable software solutions. The Java in Administration Special Interest Group, known as the JA-SIG, is leading this work (see JA-SIG.org).

The decision as to how, when, and under what circumstances an institution should develop or buy portal solutions may have strategic implications that are not obvious at first blush. Many institutions now talk about "build and buy," rather than "build or buy."

Portals Are a Hot Topic—for a Good Reason!

The EDUCAUSE Advisory Group on Administrative Information Systems and Services affirmed the importance, or even centrality, of portals at its meeting in February 2000 and again in 2001. Members of this group requested that EDUCAUSE organize a series of forums on the subjects of portals and e-business in higher education in conjunction with NACUBO—the National Association of College and University Business Officers. These forums, held in May 2000 and 2001, each with more than fifty financial and information technology professionals participating, were followed by two conferences delivered in collaboration with *Converge Magazine,* at which more than two hundred participated. Finally, EDUCAUSE and NACUBO developed this series of essays to share in the broadest way possible some of the insights and cautions that leading practitioners are discovering on the path toward formulating and implementing campus portal strategies.

The participants in these forums and conferences agree that the implementation of a portal strategy is necessary, difficult, and perilous in higher education. It is necessary because colleges and universities—to both compete and realize the full benefits of their investments in data warehouses, enterprise systems, and other elements of the campus infrastructure—will need to integrate information, services, and in-frastructure across a seamless and easy-to-navigate Web interface. This strategy is difficult and perilous because many on campus are weary and suspicious of yet another new enterprise-wide infor-mation technology initiative, and because portal initiatives, by defi-nition, require across-the-institution agreements on approach and design that are hard to achieve in loosely coupled organizations like academic institutions.

Portals Will Change How Colleges and Universities Operate

Whether or not the implementation of a campus portal strategy is difficult or perilous, participants in these recent events agree that this activity is necessary and complex. In the months ahead, col-lectively and individually, colleges and universities will have to grapple with a variety of business, organizational, technical, and pol-icy questions related to portals. For example:

- How will institutions regulate advertising on their Web sites?

- Will institutions be able to muster the political where-withal to make institution-wide decisions over IT, as well as standards to create compelling and "sticky" Web environments that create communities rather than attract surfers?

- How will institutional privacy policy be shaped to accommodate the creation of portal sites that remain compelling to different members of the campus community throughout their lives?

- Can we create either the technical or organizational infrastructure to foster what Robert Kvavik (2000) calls "cradle-to-endowment" relationships via our virtual environments.

- How will we integrate our physical and virtual sites to foster social and intellectual interactions worthy of our mission?

The challenge of a portal strategy is no less than the challenge of bringing higher education fully into the new wave of technology. This challenge, like so many we have encountered and overcome, seems to depend less on technology per se than on our ability to create a compelling vision for our institution and to galvanize the institutional will to think about how to personalize the institution for everyone in the community. It is clear in this instance that IT professionals, acting alone, will likely achieve only imperfect results. This is a daunting challenge, and the months ahead are sure to be exciting ones for us.

So What Kind of Metaphor Is Portal?

If, as I suggest, the portal is an "organizing principle" or metaphor for how institutions will organize themselves and their services in cyberspace, what are the elements of that organizing principle? The University of Washington has been developing a simple schematic that helps situate the portal within a larger technology architecture.

This schematic is helpful in serving at least two purposes. First, it situates the portal clearly within a broader context that includes other major IT initiatives, such as enterprise resource planning (ERP) systems, data warehouses, security initiatives, and the like. Second, it clearly presents the portal within a customer-centered or stakeholder-centered model of Web services or Web information delivery. The customer-centric aspect of portal strategy and design is central to understanding how new and evolving technologies can be used effectively to meet the needs of the institutions' stakeholders.

From Mass Production to Mass Personalization

As Howard Strauss (2000) makes clear, "a portal is a fundamental departure from the old entity-centric Web experience. Portals represent a basic change in the way we present web information to users and in which users use the web." In the 1960s and 1970s, our information systems were designed to support the information and transaction processing needs of such large central organizational units as registrars, personnel offices, and accounting offices. These systems provided limited flexibility. The introduction and proliferation, in the 1970s and 1980s, of fourth-generation languages made it possible for sophisticated users of information and technology to produce customized reports, again primarily for central units. On a parallel track, minicomputers performed essentially these same tasks to meet the needs of local units in disparate academic units of the institution. As Strauss indicates, the focus of technology throughout this period is on the organization entity as the "end user."

The proliferation of networks and the introduction of the World Wide Web and client-server or Web-based ERP systems in the 1990s created the potential to customize the delivery of information and services between the central and devolved organizational units of the institution. This pathway was anticipated and described by Katz and West (1992) as the "network model." At many institutions, these innovations have enabled (1) a significant devolution of organizational responsibilities, (2) enhancements to service levels between central campus units and interdependent departments, and (3) reductions in the rates of growth of administrative costs. Now, accounting professionals in academic departments can execute on-line transactions once that will be posted to institutional ledgers. At the same time, data warehouses and decision support tools make it possible for faculty members to obtain current information on their grants, budget authorizations, travel, and other administrivia.

The Web was the pivotal element of this evolution, insofar as it has allowed large numbers of campus citizens to overcome much of the "unfriendliness" inherent in most legacy systems. Some of this unfriendliness owes to the underlying complexity of institutional information, an issue that no technology is likely to overcome soon. The Web has also been liberating, making it possible for almost anyone to develop respectable, usable, and useful information pages for others to view and use. In the past five years, thousands of Web flowers have bloomed. In fact, today there are more than seventeen million distinct Web sites, a number that is growing by more than two million sites per month![1]

What's Really New?

The implication of such a remarkably accessible technology is the creation of the information frontier spirit described earlier. On college and university campuses, as the technical barriers to building Web sites fell, new campus entities entered the Web fray. As a result, a visit to most campus Web sites reveals a view of the institution most akin to that institution's organizational chart. If you are looking for a policy on how to report on NIH grants, you are likely to need to know that the sponsored research department's site will be found within the Controller's Office site, which is a part of the site maintained by the Office of the Vice Chancellor of Administration. Of course, a campus calendar that shows relevant reporting deadlines for the same type of grant might be maintained and found elsewhere on the campus Web site. The point is that "first-generation" Web tools and techniques continued our historical focus on the organizational entity as both the producer and consumer of significant institutional information and services.

Of course, organizations don't consume information, people do. The transformational wave associated with portals is being energized by the notion that organizations now must and can array their Web-based information and services in ways that are tailored to the

individual. This is a powerful shift, because, in the main, most organizations, including colleges and universities, have rarely organized
their information and service offerings—anywhere—around the
personal needs of their community members. Even the reengineering work of the 1990s focused on end-to-end processes within
broader "stovepipes." So while one can now find campus enrollment
systems that span the traditional subprocesses of admissions, financial aid administration, class registration, degree audits, and so forth,
rarely are these systems linked with systems that support marketing
for adult education, alumni systems, and other systems that support
a lifelong relationship. The new, wonderful, and challenging aspect
of Web management posed by portals is the idea of creating and
managing information systems whose primary purpose is to sustain
positive relationships between an institution's stakeholders and the
institution. That's new.

Is It Important?

The metaphor of "customer relationship management," tied so closely
to portals, is important. Devising and implementing campus portals
strategy forces the institution to begin to think of its Web site(s) as
being strategic. Most college and university leaders today agree that information technology is important. Many might not yet agree that IT
is strategic. In fact, it seems likely that the campus Web site will influence prospective applicants' early opinions about an institution—
perhaps decisively or immutably. How institutions organize their Web
sites, Web-based services, and information will affect their ability to
create communities. Throughout our history, colleges and universities
have described themselves as communities. We are "communities of
scholars," "communities of skeptics," "learning communities," and so
forth. Creative and Web-sophisticated organizations—commercial
and academic—are harnessing the evolving technologies and new
organizing principles to create powerful and compelling communities. Once created, on-line communities create and reinforce stake-

holder loyalties in much the way our traditional campuses do. The harmonious blending of a relationship-centered set of campus-based strategies with those delivered over the Web is a powerful strategy. As Greg Baroni (1999) puts it, "the debate is not about portals. It's about modernizing education, leveraging possibilities and securing a successful future for your university in a radically different environment."

It's Also About User Roles and Self-Service

The portal metaphor and organizing principle is not just about customization and personalization; it's also about roles. Colleges and universities are unique institutions that bring together multiple communities and deliver to them myriad services. This is why commercially dominant metaphors such as customer service become controversial in a higher education context. Colleges and universities are more like city-states than they are like businesses. Yes, we sell products to "consumers." We also provide day care, operate K–12 schools, provide housing and food services, dispense funds, process payrolls, deliver mail, deliver babies, operate wastewater treatment facilities, and, oh yes, educate students and pursue research and scholarship. Our communities are, by definition, diverse, and they often organize themselves along the lines of roles, interests, academic disciplines, and axes other than a consumer axis.

Two other important organizing principles around portals are well articulated by Jenny Rickard (2000): "Portal technology provides the capability to aggregate content from multiple sources, integrate ERP backbone systems into role-based self-service transactions . . . access role-based analytical information and, if desired, facilitate commercial transactions" (p. 3). Other key aspects of relationship management à la portals relate to the ideas of role-based access to information and services and to the idea of self-service.

The role-based access idea encourages future designers of campus Web sites to differentiate virtual views of the institution according to the role or roles of the Web site user. While students, faculty members, staff members, patients, and others all may use a college's or university's campus or services, they do not use these (or experience these) in the same way. Other stakeholders, such as parents and alumni, see the institution through yet another variety of lenses. Today's portal architects are crafting unique and varying top views of the institution, based on these roles. The challenge before us is to organize views that reflect the needs and wants of different stakeholders of our Web, so that again we might convert casual browsing into community building—and loyalty building—activity.

The role-based access metaphor is also powerful in the context of using portal technology as a tool to enhance institutional efficiency and productivity. Whereas the focus of much of today's discussion of portals relates predominately to the creation of Web-based student services, information, and community, one important institution has focused on the portal for administrative productivity. The portal sits at the center of what the University of California (UC) (2000) calls "a new business architecture." In essence, the UC portal strategy argues that the portal is "designed for optimal cycle-time and performance, ease of access, personalized views of information and extensive online help and training, [and that] these systems enable staff to learn about and perform a function in a single transaction. Eliminating the intermediate transactional processes between staff and the information and functions they require is the key to containing costs and reducing cumbersome bureaucracy" (p. 5).

The second powerful idea expressed by Rickard is that of self-service by the user of portal technologies. Robert Kvavik and Michael Handberg (1999) make a compelling case for self-service by describing how automated, user-initiated services can simultaneously enhance service and lower costs by transforming the college or university administrative workplace from one dominated by specialists, schooled in exotic and arcane policy and procedure, to one that supplements intuitive, self-service systems with employee generalists and, when necessary, a small cadre of specialists.

Getting There Will Be Tough

To the extent that it is true that the drive toward portals is more about securing a successful future for your institution in changing times, the effort will be arduous. As the University of California document suggests, this activity is really more about a change in the institution's approaches to managing relationships and business than it is about a change in hardware and software. To meet this challenge, colleges and universities will need to make significant investments and changes in

- Information technologies

- Business practices

- Institutional policies

- Human factors (culture, organization, incentives)

The technical challenges are daunting. Colleges and universities must strive to achieve what technologists refer to reverentially as "single sign-on." If campus information and Web-based services are to be truly easy to use and compatible with the self-service and role-based ideals described, it won't help if every component requires a separate password and user ID. At the same time, these systems need to be secure and to handily recognize an individual's authorizations, based on roles and other personal attributes. In essence, the information system must be able to know "up front" that John Doe is really John Doe and that Dr. Doe is a tenured faculty member authorized to enter the closed stacks, park in lot 3, transfer funds among three grants, and so forth. Organizing an infrastructure and institutional information and services to behave in this fashion is just hard.

Business practices will have to change. The personalization and self-service metaphors are as different from the prevailing campus business models as they are compelling. As systems are developed and placed on stream, legions of campus specialists are likely to be displaced. Whereas many will welcome the opportunity to be retrained as broadly empowered generalists, many will have difficulty coping with change and will resist such change efforts. Change management strategies will have to be developed and implemented to support the drive toward these new capabilities. Ultimately, campuses will have to make new choices of business models associated with e-business; that is, they must decide whether auctions, shopping bots, cookies, and other techniques and technologies have a place in campus business practice.

Institutional policies will be stretched into new shapes and configurations by these technologies. Will some of this activity be financed by advertising revenues enabled by the successful creation of "sticky" Web sites and "on-line communities of practice"? Should campus on-line communities be converted into buying collaboratives, and, if so, who really is a member of the "campus" community? What are the ethical, legal, and policy constraints and concerns around using student information to populate alumni profiles? Once data systems have been linked in new ways (by user roles, and so on), who really has access to what information, and for what purpose?

And, of course, the people issues will be enormous. Portal technologies, organized in ways designed to create long-term user loyalty via personalization and self-service, are inherently transformational in nature. If the technologies of the 1960s reinforced the hegemony of the central campus operating units, the technologies of the 1990s were designed to redistribute power and authority to devolved campus academic units. The new portal technologies are designed to devolve power and authority to the individual. To accomplish this, the hundreds of campus central and distributed units that have set up shop with our Web spaces will have to develop and conform to certain uniform standards of practice and design. This will not be easy. The issues raised here will also be about how one creates loyalty to an institution in environments that are completely tailored to the individual. If the first round of campus portal implementations is creating portals named MyUB, MyUW, PAWS, MyUBC, and others, the second round is likely to feature portals named MyJoe, MyMary, and MyRichard. It remains to be seen if MyPortal will foster my loyalty to YourInstitution.

The Opportunity Is Exciting

As the challenge is great, so are the opportunities. Portal technology firms have discovered higher education because they understand that colleges and universities are quintessentially relationship management enterprises. We develop *in loco parentis* relationships with people (yes, consumers) whose very roles involve receiving impressions. Faculty members, fellow students, our campuses, the teams, and every aspect of what colleges and universities do leave lasting, lifetime impressions on students. These students, when these impressions are positive ones, become lifelong members of our communities. Private firms understand this unique power. The portal challenge is a battle cry to get ourselves organized to better form these lifelong impressions. It is a belief system, a worldview, a set of approaches and technologies organized to arrange and rearrange both our front door and our rich holdings. It may be the next basis of competition between us and a new emerging knowledge "industry" or a path back to the personalized educational ideals and practices of Plato. It's our move.

This chapter expands on an essay first published in EDUCAUSE *Quarterly*, Summer 2000.

Note

1. See the survey by Netcraft [http://www.netcraft.com/survey].

References

Baroni, G. Quoted in *Into the Looking Glass: Higher Education Peeks into Portals and Sees Itself*. A Converge Special Report from the Portal Technology Symposium, 1999, p. 15.

Katz, R. N., and West, R. P. "Sustaining Excellence in the 21st Century: A Vision and Strategies for College and University Administration." CAUSE Professional Paper, 1992.

Kvavik, R. "Transforming Student Services." EDUCAUSE Quarterly, 2000, 23(2), 30–37.

Kvavik, R. B., and Handberg, M. N. "Transforming Student Services." In D. G. Oblinger and R. N. Katz (eds.), Renewing Administration: Preparing Colleges and Universities for the 21st Century. Bolton, Mass.: Anker Publishing, 1999.

Rickard, J. "Portals: Creating Lifelong Campus Citizens." Portal Technology 2000 Symposium: Portals in Higher Education. Converge Magazine supplement, Oct. 2000.

Strauss, H. "Web Portals: A Home Page Doth Not a Portal Make." Edutech Report, 2000, 15(11).

University of California, New Campus Architecture Planning Group. UC 2010: A New Business Architecture for the University of California. University of California, July 2000, p. 5. [http://uc2010.ucsd.edu].

2

Customer-Centered Resources

Ed Lightfoot and Weldon Ihrig

Web technologies offer the opportunity for our colleges and universities to move from having a historic focus on processes to being information- and communications-based institutions. The University of Washington's goal is to provide people with the information they need—when they need it, where they need it, and in a format that can easily be acted upon.

At the same time, Web technologies are generating new opportunities at a tremendous rate, and the electronically based new economy is expanding at Internet speeds. Such a rapid growth in opportunities makes it difficult to know how best to reap the benefits. Portals, e-commerce, b2b, b2c, exchanges, enterprise resource planning (ERP), mass customization, and so forth, offer a confusing array of opportunities with no clear approach or vision of how they can be integrated to meet the needs of our customers. This has led the University of Washington to envision a deceptively simple, high-level, and highly inclusive customer-centered model (shown in Figure 2.1) of how we see these pieces fitting together. The customer-centered model is useful as a way of rethinking who are the University's customers and how it can effectively use the new technologies to meet their needs.

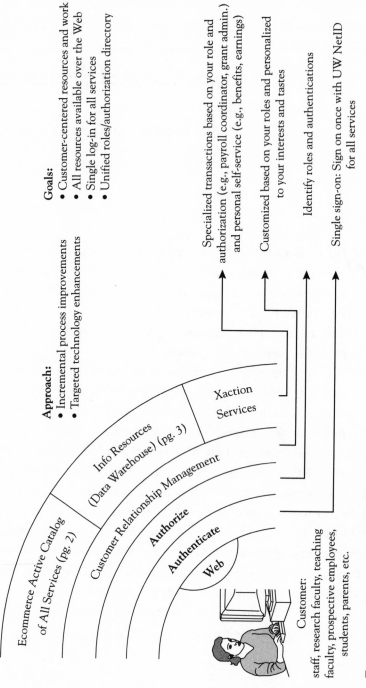

Approach:
- Incremental process improvements
- Targeted technology enhancements

Goals:
- Customer-centered resources and work
- All resources available over the Web
- Single log-in for all services
- Unified roles/authorization directory

Ecommerce Active Catalog
of All Services (pg. 2)

Info Resources
(Data Warehouse) (pg. 3)

Xaction
Services

Customer Relationship Management

Authorize

Authenticate

Web

Specialized transactions based on your role and
authorization (e.g., payroll coordinator, grant admin.)
and personal self-service (e.g., benefits, earnings)

Customized based on your roles and personalized
to your interests and tastes

Identify roles and authentications

Single sign-on: Sign on once with UW NetID
for all services

Customer:
staff, research faculty, teaching
faculty, prospective employees,
students, parents, etc.

Figure 2.1. Customer-Centered Resources

The Customer

The customer is rightfully the center of the university information model. Unlike many commercial enterprises, with simple client provider relationships, universities have a complex set of relationships with a wide variety of constituents. In fact, the term *customer* is misleading in a university context. We are using *customer* to mean the full community of individuals who have a relationship with our institution. Institutionally we tend to think in terms of separate categories for each of these relationships and separate institutional departments to service them. The new Internet-based relationships offer a unique opportunity to think more holistically about our customers and how we relate to them.

Customers interacting through the Web do not, and should not, have to think in terms of the institutional categories; they want information and services that address their needs.

The university community includes students, prospective students, extension students, certificate program students, graduate and professional students, parents, alumni, donors, sports fans, patients, referring physicians, career planners, continuing professional education students, staff members, administrators, researchers, faculty members, teaching assistants, prospective employees, and more. Indeed, of the more than a million different people each month who use the University of Washington's Web infrastructure to relate in some way with our institution, fewer than 10 percent are students, faculty members, and staff members, who make up our core campus-oriented community. Individuals are often in more than one category—such as alumni who are also patients, staff members who are also students, and parents who are also donors and sports fans. During the course of their lives, these complex relationships with the university will continue to change. It is not difficult to imagine an individual moving from the status of student in a summer extension course in middle school or high school to that of a prospective undergraduate, and then becoming an undergraduate, and then a patient, and then an alumnus, and then going on to professional school, and then to continuing education through professional certification programs, and then becoming a sports fan, downloader of lectures, legislatively active citizen, and, eventually, donor.

We have a unique opportunity to deepen and enrich these relationships over an entire lifetime: building pride, loyalty, and enhanced opportunities for the university. Many dot-coms and portals are focusing on just one of those relationships, such as that with students, alumni, or sports fans. In thinking about our strategies for the new economy, as well as new learning and health care environments, it is important to develop an approach that is inclusive and discovers and even creates synergies between the different relationships, rather than fragmenting them into different silos or dealing with them monolithically.

The Web

The Web is the universal lens through which we will offer access to all of the university's information resources and the transactions that accomplish work. A strategy that is not based on this principle will tend to create barriers to access. For example, ERP systems or legacy systems that do not provide rich complex access to information resources via the Web will need to be modified or enhanced to do so.

Traditionally, the Web has been thought of as a way of publishing static content—an electronic hyperlinked version of printed materials. It is now time to rethink the Web and view it as a flexible, active, and personalized transaction-oriented service environment that can offer content and services that recognize an individual's interests and needs. To accomplish this will require a set of policy and technology infrastructure services that don't yet exist—in anything other than test bed form—at most of our institutions.

Authentication

Many universities are just beginning to broadly implement the concept of a single network ID to provide a uniform way of identifying a user for a wide variety of Web-based services. Taking this concept one step further, we are proposing the assignment of a single university ID that will give an individual access to the full range of university services over his or her lifetime. This ID can replace and bridge across the proliferation of IDs currently in use: employee IDs, student IDs, alumni numbers, and, most especially, the problematic social security number still used at many institutions.

Obviously there are many policy and implementation issues to consider in making this viable. If we are to offer services that involve sensitive information protected by privacy laws, transactions that represent potential liabilities for the institution, or transactions that, if compromised, would affect the credibility and good reputation of the institution, we need to set up processes and technologies that balance security with the level of risk.

For example, when the universal ID is assigned, we need to use processes to ensure that we are indeed providing the ID and password in a way that is appropriate to security requirements. The level of authentication that may be appropriate for a high school student seeking admission may be quite different from the security required for some administrative transactions, for a patient, or for an emergency room physician. Use of a universal ID, more importantly, will help us think more institutionally and systematically about our relationships as part of a university community.

Authorization

Once the infrastructure has authenticated the user and has provided the appropriate level of assurance that the individual is indeed who he or she logged in as, we need to understand what the roles, relationships, and authorizations are that are associated with that individual. These roles and authorizations are often contained within separately managed authorization files associated with each system or service.

As more transactional services are offered over the Web, this fragmented approach to authorizations and roles will become extremely cumbersome to administer. The ideal administrative approach will be a decentralized, self-service model using electronic forms. All requests for authorization will follow similar, self-managed review and approval processes used for all other administrative reviews, such as purchases and personnel requests. This workflow management approach is an important component that allows for the centralized management of authorization in a decentralized manner.

Another key component of the authorization infrastructure is the concept of a person registry that tracks individuals and their associated relationships with the institution. Many universities do not yet consolidate different roles, such as that of alumni, student, staff member, and faculty member, into a single identity. It is essential to do this if we are to offer the well-focused yet integrated and facilitating view of the institution to an individual.

Relationship Management—the Portal

The portal depends on the authentication and authorization infrastructure for its power. Logging in with the university ID, the individual is authenticated, and the authorization system can recognize the full set of relationships and authorizations an individual has with the institution.

The portal can then build a default view of the Web-based information and services appropriate for the individual's relationships with the institution, and the individual can further personalize that view, based on his or her interests and needs. The portal, or relationship manager, will then keep track of the changing relationships and personalizations over time. This is a very powerful concept that will allow institutions over time to build communities of interest and deepen the relationships that currently exist between individuals and the university.

Services

The services offered through the portal will reflect the full range of activities of the institution: teaching, learning, research, library services, public service, patient care, entertainment, the arts, and so forth.

Concepts such as "My Work" (a personalized dashboard of transaction-oriented services necessary for the activities of an administrator or researcher), or "My Studies," which reflects the individualized course content and activities for a student (including the educational outreach/distance learning student), or "My Admission" application, or "My Employment" application, are ways of thinking about how to organize these services within the portal.

Business-to-business e-commerce services can offer a catalog of both university and external vendor goods and services appropriate to an individual's role within the institution.

Business-to-customer services can offer a wide array of targeted services tailored to the interests and needs of the individual. Avoiding blanket advertising and offering tailored services within the commercialization policies of the institution can be accomplished, based on the roles and user profiles offered by the portal. For example, a graduating senior can be assisted in planning for the graduation ceremony, renting the gown, planning for travel, and arranging for the lodging of his or her visiting family.

Community-building tools allow subscription to, participation in, or setting up of discussion groups, information feeds, or shared activities of interest to the individual.

These tailored service offerings are all possible because of the infrastructure that recognizes who you are through your authenticated university ID, what your roles and authorizations are, what information you use and subscribe to, and what your personalized interests and activities are.

The Challenges

The challenges associated with implementing such a vision are enormous, but they have the potential to be transformational in the same way that so much of what we do today is being transformed by Web technologies and the new economy. A demonstration that reflects some of the University of Washington's thinking about future services can be found at http://www.washington.edu/protos/myuw/demo.

We hope this vision and approach will be helpful as you sort through your own unique campus requirements. We would appreciate receiving your thoughts and feedback about the model or the approaches embedded in our MyUW demo. Please e-mail Ed Lightfoot at elight@cac.washington.edu.

3

Customer Relationship Management
A Vision for Higher Education

Gary B. Grant and Greg Anderson

E ducational institutions worldwide are undergoing fundamental shifts in how they operate and interact with their "customers": students, alumni, donors, faculty members, and staff members. Kotler and Fox (1995) state that "the best organization in the world will be ineffective if the focus on 'customers' is lost. First and foremost is the treatment of individual students, alumni, parents, friends, and each other (internal customers). Every contact counts!"

During the mid-1980s and the late 1990s, many colleges and universities began restructuring and reengineering their operating processes to cut costs and become more efficient while responding to increased competition. Yet these organizations also realized that building the in-house technology necessary to achieve these goals was expensive, difficult, and time-consuming. As a result, many turned to enterprise resource planning (ERP) applications. These applications helped them automate and optimize their internal business processes—in areas such as finance, grants management, student information, enrollment, inventory management, and human resources—and freed them from some of the minutia found in day-to-day operations.

The focus is currently shifting from improving internal operations to concentrating more on customers. Higher education customers are demanding more attention and immediate service—that is, "Internet time." Proactive institutions are now adjusting their practices by refocusing their efforts externally. Because of the need to concentrate more on customers, many institutions are once again turning to technology—this time to customer relationship management (CRM) software. Similar to ERP, CRM solutions focus on automating and improving processes, although the focus is on front office areas, such as recruiting, marketing, customer service, and support. CRM goes several steps further than ERP by helping institutions maximize their customer-centric resources.

What Is CRM?

CRM is both a business strategy and a set of discrete software tools and technologies, with the goal of reducing costs, increasing revenue, identifying new opportunities and channels for expansion, and improving customer value, satisfaction, profitability, and retention. CRM software applications embody best practices and employ advanced technologies to help organizations achieve these goals. CRM focuses on automating and improving the institutional processes associated with managing customer relationships in the areas of recruitment, marketing, communication management, service, and support. CRM takes a very customer-centric view of the entire customer life cycle, which means that a CRM business strategy places the customer at the center of the organization's universe.

From the perspective of the customer, a CRM business strategy allows interaction with the college or university from a single entity that has a complete understanding of their unique status. In the case of a student, this might be seen through the interaction with and between the admissions, registration, financial aid, student accounts, and housing offices. For a faculty or staff member, a CRM business strategy would optimize interaction with departments administering benefits, payroll, staff training, information technology (IT), or facilities. From the perspective of the college or university, the CRM business strategy provides a clear and complete picture of each individual and all the activities pertaining to the individual.

But what are the tangible CRM advantages, and what do they really mean to the customers? This question is probably easiest answered through an example of how CRM activities are being applied in the service industries in a scenario not far from the actual process of a customer on a higher education campus. The following example addresses a customer calling the telephone company and reaching a customer service representative who knows his or her account and service status immediately upon answering the call.

A telephone feature identifies the caller, cues the caller to enter a billing number, and then exchanges data with the company's customer call center software. Automatic call distribution (ACD) software then routes the call to a customer service representative. The customer service representative then uses software designed specifically to answer customer questions. This differs from administrative systems, which are designed to process transactions. The CRM business strategy applied in this example allows the customer to call one number for all his or her needs, enabling the service request to be completed in one call. In this case, the customer service representative is starting the interaction from a position of knowledge. The technologies employed include telephony, ACD, data warehouse, intelligent scripting, and interfaces with such legacy systems as billing. These technologies are all existing and mature applications and have been integrated to streamline the delivery of service.

Why Implement a Higher Education CRM Business Strategy?

Higher education is in much the same position with CRM as it was in with ERP—just far enough behind the commercial sector to gain from the lessons learned and the maturation of the technology.

Departments and offices work as separate entities in many colleges and universities today. Faced with divisional boundaries, it is often very difficult for these different institutional functions to focus on their customers in a coordinated fashion. By providing a common platform for customer communication and interaction, CRM solutions aim to eliminate the organizational stovepipes that hamper proactive customer interaction. CRM applications are also designed to increase the effectiveness of staff members who interact with customers or prospects. The use of CRM applications can lead to improved customer responsiveness and a more comprehensive view of the entire "cradle-to-grave" customer life cycle. CRM solutions that tie directly into ERP systems are particularly powerful because institutions can take customers through a closed-looped set of well-defined steps and processes to satisfy their needs. Whereas CRM applications provide the framework for embodying, promoting, and executing best practices in customer-facing activities, ERP provides the backbone, resources, and operational applications to make organizations more efficient in achieving these goals.

Most exciting of all is CRM's ability to promote and enable e-business, which is the seamless, Web-based collaboration between an institution and its customers, suppliers, and partners. CRM applications track and manage interactions and transactions with various customers across multiple channels, including the Web. For institutions with a high degree of personal interaction, such as admissions recruiters or development officers, CRM can extend these channels to the Web by providing a framework for managing the interactions and transactions. CRM can also enable purchase of products or services on-line, and provide Web-based services and support, all personalized for the individual customer.

An Example of CRM in Higher Education

Emerging CRM processes and technologies will drive the growth of new types of resources and services. The following example highlights the opportunity to implement a CRM business strategy to support the student during the admissions and recruitment process.

Marketing and campaign management processes and applications can support both targeted admission recruitment and fundraising. For example, the institution may have an enrollment goal to recruit out-of-state students and minorities and to increase the number of students pursuing health careers. An institution would target specific groups, using data analysis to determine which prospects are most likely to apply and why. A personalized mailing campaign would then be launched using both e-mail and traditional mail. Within each mailing, prospects would be given a personal identification code for access to the university. All prospects not responding by any channel (Web, e-mail, phone, fax, or other) would be sent follow-up e-mails.

A prospect receives the e-mail three days before the receipt of the paper letter. The prospect then activates the hyperlink and is linked to the university's recruitment Web page. The prospect is requested to enter his or her personal identification code and then is linked to a personalized home page and portal. The Web page is customized, based on interests known from the search data. For example, if the prospect is interested in sports or band, links to the university's athletic department or music club Web pages are provided. Or if the prospect listed health as an occupational choice, there are links to health departments' Web pages. Finally, there are standard links provided to all prospective students, such as admissions application procedures and forms, financial aid information, and scholarship search programs. The prospect navigates through the site, completes an electronic inquiry card, and requests information on physical therapy programs and financial aid. The university then monitors the prospect's responses and initiates follow-up communications, as appropriate.

The Impact of CRM on the Higher Education Enterprise

Emerging CRM processes and technologies will drive the growth of new types of resources and services. Within the higher education enterprise, much of this new functionality will be focused in the student area. This exciting new level of student-related functionality and performance will have an impact on students as well as on the administrative staff and management, the faculty, and the institution as a whole. A look at each of the areas affected follows.

Students

Today's systems have little to offer students, particularly the new breed of technology-savvy students who want to be more in control of their learning environment. Today's students demand a higher level of access to information about their options, their performance, and their future. They also demand that technology resources be an integral part of their learning experience. The standard for access to faculty and student services will change as students come to expect virtual access to faculty and student services resources. The old ways of interacting with students will become untenable—like expecting them to line up for hours when instead they can choose an institution that can meet their needs on their own terms, on their schedule, with virtual support systems.

Administrators

A CRM business strategy for a college's or university's administrative system would also introduce a true self-service system that empowers the administrative team to rethink the investment of administrative resources in institutional services. By shifting responsibility for information maintenance to students and faculty members, and empowering them to complete relevant processes and securely access vital information, the administrative staff can focus on more productive, rewarding, and satisfying activities—such as making personal connections with students and helping them plan for the future.

Faculty Members

Today's systems provide little value for faculty members. In many institutions, there is a complete disconnect between student services and instructional programs. This disconnect is often mirrored in the rift between administrative and academic computing. In the new learning environment, faculty and student services are closely linked, dynamically sharing resources and strategies to enable student learning. Envision a time when faculty members can securely access student learning profiles assembled in the admissions process to prepare custom learning options for students who are having difficulty. Imagine a process whereby a faculty member can make immediate student referrals to key support programs on campus—even when working at home. Finally, with a system that is dynamically linked with students, faculty curriculum planners can develop an accurate picture of which technology resources truly make a difference in student learning.

Advancement

Fundraising is increasingly important in higher education. The objective is to "sell" the organization's mission to donors. Success is measured by how often gift-giving solicitation results in "taking an order." Solicitation is often done by volunteers who view fundraising as sales. In the CRM approach, individualized techniques are applied to prospective donors whose connections to the institution have been established through some other relationship, such as that of an athletic supporter or music lover. The CRM approach identifies, selects, and generates lists of targeted customers with current information to build constituencies that continue gift giving long after they or their sons or daughters have graduated. These donors consider their gifts to be investments in values that are important to them. Furthermore, other people value these donors' views, making them articulate advocates of the institution. Using CRM, the entire institution, not just a small group of volunteer telephone solicitors, is involved and organized around fundraising. Using technology to know that a donor's last contribution was used to purchase football helmets is of great value when soliciting donations the next time. The ultimate goal is to entice donors to contribute in the future without direct solicitation.

The Institution

CRM delivers a new conceptual and structural framework for directing institutional activities to attract and retain its various customers. Following are ways in which all customers of the institution can benefit from increased access to information and services.

- Students, alumni, faculty members, and staff members can access and update information from any Web-enabled device, anywhere in the world.

- The evolution from point-to-point integration between applications to a single institution-wide database with integrated business rules and a workflow process library will blur the distinction between student, finance, alumni, and human resource systems.

- The needs of the customer base become the focus rather than the rigid process structure that is the focus of today's systems.

- Administrative systems are seamlessly integrated with instructional computing and communications systems.

Most important is the ability of a truly robust set of institutional processes and tools to bring the entire institution together around its people. The work of higher education should be focused on the people it serves, not on its administrative systems.

What Is the Return on Investment (ROI) of a CRM Business Strategy?

The benefits of implementing a CRM business strategy are far-reaching. Because CRM activities and technologies are fairly new to higher education, the best benchmarks come from the commercial sector. They include

- Up to 42 percent increase in revenue

- Up to 35 percent decrease in cost of sales

- Up to 80 percent decrease in order errors

- Up to 25 percent reduction in the length of sales cycle

- Up to 2 percent increase in margins

- Up to 20 percent increase in customer satisfaction ratings[1]

For colleges and universities, these could translate into

- Increased revenue through improved recruitment and retention

- Reduced recruitment costs

- Improved customer service

- Quicker yield conversions

- Improved customer satisfaction

Many colleges and universities entered into ERP implementations with the goal of improving customer service. To some degree, service improvements were realized, but not because of improved support of customer interaction. These gains were realized through improved processing speed and better data. The investment in CRM enables an institution to better capitalize on its ERP investment. The CRM business strategy and associated technologies target facilitating the direct customer interaction. These processes and technologies can aid the institution in gaining a total view of its customers and can help implement activities to capitalize on this knowledge.

For a college or university to actualize the potential for these processes and technologies, it should first determine its vision for customer service and the relationships it wants to foster, and then it should break the implementation of the vision into small manageable projects. For example, an institution should implement marketing and campaign management first in the admissions office and then expand its use into advancement, human resources, and payroll. Contact center applications may first be implemented in IT and then rolled out to student services, admissions, and other areas.

Conclusion

Faced with widespread economic, technological, and cultural change, academic institutions are looking to enhance the value and effectiveness of their existing customer relationships, while attracting new and loyal customers. As institutions begin embracing e-business and e-learning, the driving forces behind CRM will become even stronger.

The notion of effective customer information management as a productivity issue is being replaced by the need for effective customer management as a competitive advantage. Tomorrow's systems will go far beyond productivity-related features (such as Web-based student registration) to the development of customer information as a strategic advantage. The concept of students, alumni, faculty members, and staff members as "customers" will become a competitive imperative with profound impact on how colleges and universities attract, retain, and serve customers of all types.

Note

1. From a survey of 295 companies by Insight Technologies Group.

Reference

Kotler, P., and Fox, K. *Strategic Marketing for Educational Institutions*. Englewood Cliffs, N.J.: Prentice Hall, 1995.

4

All About Web Portals
A Home Page Doth Not a Portal Make

Howard Strauss

The World Wide Web continues to be the preeminent application on the Internet because it has regularly reinvented itself. In fact, for most people, the World Wide Web has become synonymous with the Internet. With the introduction of Web portals, the Web is in the process of reinventing itself once again. This change may prove to be more far-reaching than any other change to hit the Web, and it will change the way that university and corporate Web pages are built, the organizational structures used to build them, and the fundamental way that people use the Web. Portals are not a fad or a new name for something that we've been doing all along. They will turn the Web from an institution-centric repository of information and applications to a dynamic user-centric collection of everything useful to a particular person in a particular role. Instead of a single home page that proclaims identically to all who visit how grand the institution is, portals will give nearly every user a customized, personalizable, unique Web page.

Every information technology (IT) vendor and many IT professionals are rushing to produce portalware and portal-like Web pages without fully understanding the scope of a portal undertaking for an institution or even really understanding what a Web portal is or should do. At the 2000 Detroit Auto Show, Ford's former CEO, Jacques Nasser, said, "We will do nothing short of transforming our cars and trucks into a portal for the Internet." Cars cannot be a Web portal. They might access a portal, but Mr. Nasser is using *portal* to mean any place where you can access the Web. Peter Granoff of Wine.com says that they will become *the* wine portal. Mr. Granoff probably means that everything you'll want to do with wine will be at Wine.com and it will remember your preferences. That's at least somewhat portal-like. Digiscents is building a Snortal, a Web portal for interactive smelling experiences. CampusPipeline.com wants to build the student Web portal for your university, and dozens of companies, including IBM (Enterprise Information Portal), Oracle (Enterprise Portal), PeopleSoft, Blackboard, Pearson, and many others offer portal products. Within two years virtually every software vendor will offer some portal product or will assure you that their application will at least run with whatever portal you choose.

Beyond this group of dot-coms that would sell you their portalware are hundreds of sites that vie to be your free portal to the Web, such as Netscape's NetCenter, Excite's My Excite, Yahoo's My Yahoo, AltaVista's My AltaVista, and many others. Soon, almost anything you put the word "My" in front of will produce a portal-like Web page—for example, My.ragingbull.com, My.ticketmaster.com, and My.propertyline.com.

What's a Portal?

With so many portals out there and so many vendors hawking portalware, one might think that there is at least a firm agreement on what portals are. In fact, there are many confusing and often contradictory definitions. Some people even believe that just putting the word *portal* prominently on their home page makes it a portal. After all, with enough links, and especially a link to a search engine, any home page can give you access to much of the Web. Isn't that a portal?

It is useful to divide portals into two groups: horizontal portals, or HEPs (Horizontal Enterprise Portals, also called megaportals), and vertical portals, or VEPs (Vertical Enterprise Portals). A horizontal portal is a public Web site that attempts to provide its users with all the services they might need. NetCenter and MyExcite are examples of horizontal portals. All HEPs include shopping, weather, stock prices, news, search engines, chat groups, horoscopes, and so forth, and they all urge you to make their page the first page you see when you use the Web. They allow you to personalize the page you see by selecting the cities for which you'd like the weather, choosing the stocks and news sources you'd like to display, altering the appearance of the Web page, and much more. Some HEPs let you do extensive personalization, allowing you to build multiple stock portfolios and see frequently updated valuations. Typically, but not always, the personalization is held in Web cookies that are stored on your local computer. Accessing a HEP from another computer loses all of your personalization. HEPs almost always include advertising that pays for the portal, and their goal is to attract as many eyeballs as possible.

HEPs do not give academic or corporate employees access to everything they really need on the Web. Much of what an employee of any kind needs on the Web is specific to where he or she works and his or her role in that organization. Employees need university calendars that include university holidays and events, access to financial reports, the status of the tasks they are working on, organization charts, benefits information, and much more. Different people need quite different information, depending on their role. Students, for example, need to see their course and exam schedules, the books they have borrowed from the library, their grades and grade point average, their financial aid status, information about their extracurricular activities, and so forth. Prospective students, their parents, the parents of enrolled students, alumni, faculty members, scholars from other institutions, and vendors to the university all have very different needs for Web information from the same organization. Horizontal portals have no way of offering that kind of organization-specific information because they are not connected to any organization's data sources except their own. Only your own organization or organizations can really deliver access to all the Web information you need, and even then, much of the information you need will be outside your university, such as your very important TIAA/CREF or other retirement plan information.

A VEP is a portal that delivers organization-specific information in a user-centric way. A university VEP should also deliver all the information a HEP delivers. Whereas a HEP looks the same to all who first enter it, a VEP looks quite different. Unlike a HEP, a VEP requires authentication for access. When a user logs on to a VEP, it produces a customized portal page, tailored to the user who logged on. It knows a great deal about the user who logged on because the user is a member of the organization that produced the VEP. It knows, for example, what cohort a user belongs to (for example, student, faculty, staff), what role a user plays (for example, help desk manager, department chair, lacrosse team member), what projects a user is involved with, how many vacation days a user has taken this year, and much more. The information that no HEP could possibly know can be used to customize a portal page so that even for a first approximation it contains all the Web information a user would normally use. Naturally, that would look quite different for different users, and, of course, as with HEPs, the user can personalize the initial portal page.

CPAD

Ultimately, a vertical university portal should be a single CPAD— a customized, personalized, adaptive desktop. Customization is done by the portal software's knowledge of an authenticated portal user. When you authenticate to a vertical portal, it can gain access to a great deal of information about you and present you with a customized portal page. Every user of a vertical portal should see a different customized initial portal page, since no two people are exactly alike. The portal's customization engine that resides on the portal's application server is responsible for determining each user's roles, responsibilities, workflow, and the information that that person is authorized to access. As this information changes, the portal changes the customized portal view that it presents to you. Better customization makes for a better portal. HEPs have little or no customization, since they initially have access to very little information about you. And one hopes that they don't have access to your personal university data.

Even the best customization will not be able to give you the perfect portal. Everyone works differently and has different needs and desires. A portal needs to let you personalize the portal pages and needs to both remember and let you undo personal changes that you make to the customized portal. At the very least, you need to be able to subscribe and unsubscribe to channels and alerts, set backgrounds, colors, fonts, and the position of everything on the portal, set application parameters, create and edit profiles, add and remove links, and in dozens of ways make the portal a perfect fit for the way in which you do your everyday work. Not only should the portal give you ready access to all of the information and applications that you commonly use, it should also give you that access in the way that is best suited to you.

A portal should be adaptive. It should know your schedule and workflow and present you with the right information at the right time. It might know, for example, that you create your capital budgets in the spring and do employee performance evaluations in February. The right tools to do these tasks should appear at the right time. It should also sense the way you work and suggest ways to facilitate what you are doing. If it sees you leaving the portal often to use some remote application, it should help you add it to the portal or just add it itself.

Finally, the portal should be your computer desktop. It should be *the* application that appears first on your screen and in most cases should replace everything else on your computer desktop. From a user point of view, the portal will become the computer. Users would do e-mail, text processing, budgeting, system design, and all of the work they might need to do via the portal. Looking at the screen desktop of such a user, the only thing that would ever appear would be the portal and the things obtained via the portal. This vision of a portal as a customized, personalized, adaptive desktop or CPAD is just a bit down the road, and it is where we should be going. With a CPAD, the operating system you use, whether Mac, PC, Unix, or Linux, is not obvious or important to a user. Neither is the hardware. A CPAD being accessed from a wireless laptop, palm-sized computer, Web appliance, Web phone, or intelligent watch, would be automatically customized to fit that environment.

What's in a VEP?

A VEP is a single page with access to all the information and applications a user commonly needs. It will contain alerts, navigation tabs and icons, directories, graphics, and links.

Because a VEP should be *the* place for a user to obtain Web information, it must include an advanced search capability. The search should include the ability to search all of the Web, only the Web pages of the user's organization, the information on the actual portal page the user is viewing, or only information related to specific channels on the portal.

Most of a portal's functionality will be contained in small window-like areas called channels.

Channels

Although a portal is much more than a dynamic list of links, it will definitely contain many links. Almost all of the links will be contained in channels. Channels contain specific information and/or applications, such as stocks, weather, benefits, search, calendars, and so forth. Often, the channels are arranged newspaper-style in columns, with several channels appearing in each column. When a portal first appears, its customization engine subscribes a user to the most appropriate channels. The contents of a channel can be personalized, and its size, appearance, and position within the portal page can also be personalized. In addition, a user can subscribe and unsubscribe to any channel he or she is authorized to access. Not all such channels will necessarily appear when the portal is first viewed.

A channel gives a user access to specific information. One way to do that is with links, which channels do use, but filling a channel totally with links turns it into little more than a dynamic bookmark or favorites list. Traversing hypertext links for commonly needed information makes for a poorly designed portal. A channel needs to display the actual data or part of the actual application a user needs, not a link to it.

Suppose a department manager needs to track the amount of money left in her capital budget. She would like the budget channel on her portal to display that amount right on the portal page. These tiny data windows within a channel that display small but important parts of critical data are called *data cameos*. A channel can also display *application cameos*. These are small but important parts of an application. An application cameo enables a portal user to run a small bit of an application within a portal channel. When appropriate, the user might enter data into an application text box within the application cameo to produce some result. For a searching channel, there would be no link to a search engine. Instead, there would be a text box into which a user would type his or her search request. There would also be a number of buttons and switches to select the kind of search needed. Depending upon the results, they might be displayed within the portal channel or on a new Web page. For example, a common search that many people do is to enter a name to look up a university phone number and e-mail address. In this case, a user would just enter the person's name, and the corresponding e-mail address and phone number would appear on the portal page with the search channel.

Channels can also contain Web cameos that are similar to data and application cameos but have as their source a Web page or Web application. Links should be used only when it is impossible or impractical to use cameos.

How to Proceed

Many universities are considering what they call student portals or course portals or financial information portals. Although starting with a portal that has a limited constituency may make sense, the goal of a university should be to move as quickly as possible to a single portal that serves everyone: students, faculty members, staff members, alumni, parents of students, prospective students, trustees, donors, and anyone else who would access a university home page.

Before you proceed, look at what others have done. Even using the common free horizontal portals will give you many ideas of what's possible and what works well or poorly.

The portal you build or buy (or, most probably, buy and build onto) should have a single sign-on. From a single portal, most users will access many applications that today require separate authentication. A user needs to authenticate once to a portal and then have the portal authenticate the user to all authorized applications as necessary.

It should also be easy for IT folks and users to add and delete channels, even channels that are far outside the realm of your university.

The Web is about to change again. Portals represent an enormous change to both the user and the IT staff, but it is a change that will add great value to all university information and applications, make your users and IT staff members much more efficient and productive, and provide a compelling, entertaining, and educational experience for all who visit your new user-centric Web site.

5

E-Business in Higher Education

Robert B. Kvavik

E-business for universities is first and foremost about improving service to their diverse clientele.[1] New e-business models promise to radically change the service culture of the university and greatly improve the efficiency and effectiveness of service delivery. Especially noteworthy is service customization, or "marketing to one." In effect, each client is afforded an opportunity to view the institution in ways that make the most sense to the client, as opposed to a more generic and group view orchestrated by the institution.

Second, e-business is about community building, and especially the development and nurturing of learning communities. By *learning community*, I refer to groups of people engaged in collective inquiry on the Web. Paul Shrivastava (1999) notes that "learning occurs from interaction in the network and from learning materials and databases. In work settings, learning communities are also 'communities of practice' that consist of knowledge workers engaged in problem solving. They include multiple forms of learning and engagement from formal coursework, research and scholarship, work practices, and informal information scanning and sharing."

The Web creatively links together the university's many learning communities (alumni, current student body, the general public) and affords new opportunities and ways to communicate, educate, and generate support (such as chat groups, e-mail and e-forums, personal links and listservs, ride boards, elections, and surveys).

Third, e-business promises to change how we teach and learn. Computer-mediated and interactive instruction to Web-linked learning communities, together with new public/private teaching partnerships (division of labor), will encourage and support changes in the conduct and organization of teaching and learning. Information technology will present the possibility of greater customization of courses and programs, combined with enhanced flexibility of delivery.

Fourth, e-business is far more about strategy and business redesign than technology. The Internet and the browser are tools that make e-business possible, but new business strategies and models of service delivery are needed to make it successful and to capture the imagination and loyalty of students, faculty members, and staff members.

Because e-business has the potential to affect a wide variety of university services and how we teach, it is worthwhile to identify those areas most likely to be affected, as well as opportunities for, barriers to, and measurable benefits and costs of implementation. Also addressed are areas that are most promising to pursue.

Service delivery and teaching need to be realigned and/or redesigned around the Internet and the use of portals. Roles, responsibilities, and reporting relationships change markedly. Note that such changes have significant organizational and human resources (HR) implications, which must be addressed in a comprehensive and strategic manner as well.

What Does E-Business Encompass?

E-business encompasses a vast array of activity, including the following:

- Distribution of information (content distribution) and communication—for example, Web searching, news, reference tools and digitized library material, e-mail, and chat groups

- Education and training—for example, technology-enhanced learning (TEL), Web-based courses and testing, video streaming, course delivery to distributed locations, multi-institutional and consortia-based education programs, and health care delivery

- Provision of staff and student services via the Web and a common portal, providing referrals and dynamic links to other ISPs—creating, in effect, a one-stop service

- Optimization of business processes through linked transactions, automation, and self-help—for example, on-line applications and payment of admissions fees, on-line purchasing, and loan programs

- On-line, collaborative research

- Electronic grant and development initiatives

- Customization of service delivery

- Electronic authentication/identification

- Selling and buying of goods and services

- Extension of market reach to new and global markets via distance education

- Promotion of brand awareness and loyalty

- Building of communities, especially learning communities

- Management of relationships and coordination of activities with business partners, as well as redefinition of business relationships

- Management and support of relationships with the university's many constituencies

- Management of risk and compliance

Why Is the University Challenged by E-Business? Issues and Contradictions

Popular belief suggests that the traditional university is under enormous pressure from private corporations (and some public institutions) that use e-business to start new universities in the world of virtual space. Unfettered by the need for classrooms, libraries, dormitories, and football teams, and able to recruit and employ a nonresident and highly competitive faculty, these corporations (now over five hundred in number) presumably have a competitive advantage in market reach and low overhead. For-profit education companies such as the Apollo Group and DeVRY, Inc., focus on career-oriented education in fast-growing fields such as business, electronics, applied arts, and health care. Their enrollments are growing to where they hold nearly 2 percent of the overall market share and they are growing at over 10 percent yearly (Blustain, Goldstein, and Lozier, 1998). They have at this time a predictable stream of earnings, demand for their programs is solid, and they are innovative in the development of curricula and education delivery that appeals to both students and employers. Other players include corporate universities, such as Motorola, GM, and McDonald's, which educate their own employees, and mega-universities, such as the Open University, which service well over 164,000 students in over forty countries. And recently, Michael Saylor announced that he would use $100 million of his software profits to create free online education provided by thousands of educators (*New York Times*, Mar. 2000).

Popular belief, while often compelling, is often simplistic and requires further scrutiny if we are to understand external challenges to the traditional university. More precisely, what is it about the traditional university that places it at risk in the e-business environment? Concomitantly, recognizing factors that put the university at risk, how does the university adjust to and mitigate these risks? It should be noted from the outset that e-business is more than the virtual university. The use of the browser and Internet can be applied as easily to educational processes as it can to the hosting of university administrative and business processes.

Puryear and Melnicoff (1999) offer insight from the private sector. They recognize five realities that affect the competitiveness of traditional businesses in the new business environment. I extend their arguments to the university and add to them.

Vertical Integration

Vertical integration occurs when "all elements of the business are managed and produced within the business/corporation and where nothing is outsourced" (Puryear and Melnicoff, 1999). Alternatively, horizontal integration involves the location and integration of the best of breed services, within or without the institution, which provide more cost-effective similar services. Because in using the Internet the cost of collaboration and interaction is low, e-business often makes it cheaper to collaborate with external vendors than to own and produce all aspects of the business.

Numerous e-business vendors are now in the market, successfully serving a variety of functions. In the area of on-line admissions we find, for example, CollegeNet and EMBARK. Varsitybooks.com and Textbooks.com sell textbooks. On-line procurement is available from CommerceOne and Ariba. SallieMae, eStudentLoan, and other, similar, firms are providing a variety of services in areas of bill presentment and the management of loans and collections. All of these can be integrated into the institution's Web site.

Universities are reluctant to outsource for a variety of reasons. Political factors, loyalty to existing employees and processes, and inertia restrain the integration of external vendors into the service calculus. In the absence of comparable data, the belief persists at many higher education institutions that internal units can do the job better, which may well be the case. But it is my belief that the trend will be to outsource. Cherished management of such perceived core business as issuance of transcripts, financial aid, and course delivery may well be transferred to external vendors in the future. All parties agree to operate within a horizontal and integrated business arrangement, which is designed by the university in collaboration with external vendors, in the interest of providing the highest level of service to the customer.

Another related dilemma is the hierarchical and silo structure of some university service units. The challenge is to build seamless structures without centers that are highly networked, flexible, and easily modified. Services must be less bureaucratic, meaning they must involve paperless transactions, fewer forms, and no lengthy approvals. Certification processes must become simpler, and in some instances, we must accept more self-certification (for example, placing greater responsibility and accountability in the hands of those we serve).

Some services need to be shared more than is now the case—for example, financial and human resource (HR) functions. Many small departments use part-time and rather amateur employees to manage financial and HR functions. The new enterprise systems permit greater efficiencies in these areas and they demand more expertise if their planning and assessment functions are to be used to full advantage.

Centrality of Physical Assets Versus Knowledge-Based Products

Formerly, for private businesses, the creation of knowledge was a cost of doing business and an ultimate source of value, but not a source of revenue. Revenue was generated by the sale of goods and services. The world is very different today, as knowledge has become a very valuable commodity. It is increasingly the business of the nation and the business community.

The creation of knowledge has long been the business of the university and a source of revenue through the dissemination of information as well as royalties on patents and copyrights. Physical assets remain critical to providing high-quality research and instruction as well as building community and loyalty to the institution. However, e-business allows intangible assets to be leveraged across a wider customer base, and that is a challenge for the university. For example, it is no longer necessary to co-locate services with physical assets, such as distance education or Web-based student services. Physical library holdings will give way, in part, to efficient and sophisticated access to massive amounts of diverse and rich electronic information.

Perhaps most important is the possibility of syndicating courses and course materials through on-line instruction (see Werbach, 2000). Long prevalent in the media industry, syndication presents a major opportunity in the digital environment. Infinite numbers of people can use and reuse modular information distributed through thousands of independent distribution points (Web sites). Universities can syndicate content by drawing and archiving materials from numerous partners. A wonderful example is the Distributed Learning Network, sponsored by the Midwest Higher Education Consortium (MHEC), which is a consortium of universities providing digital course materials for use throughout the consortium. Universities can also choose to deliver these courses to students throughout the world. UCLA Extension has formed an alliance with the Home Education Network to distribute their courses via CD-ROM on-line and via satellite. Unext.com has partnered with Stanford, Chicago, Columbia, Carnegie Mellon, and the London School of Economics to develop course materials for a "global university."

The universities must decide how to partner, with whom, and what role to play. Will they be primarily providers of content to syndicators and their distributors, or will they choose to syndicate not only educational material, but also, for example, advising access to library materials.

Information-based products are scalable, and each item that you sell costs no more than the last one you delivered. Costs approach zero after an initial investment in research and development. The first business unit to capture a percentage of the market locks in the standard and a majority of the business. This argument is especially familiar in discussions of the merits of the virtual university.

The former assertion is probably a myth, as the ongoing costs of quality education and service and course delivery on distributed systems remain as high as ever or higher. However, the services do scale and the quality of services delivered is presumably better. And as I previously noted, opportunities for syndication of reusable digital course materials is continually increasing.

Student services provides a good example, as does access to library information. The University of Minnesota student Web site receives more than thirteen million hits a month and three million pages of information are downloaded. The numbers continue to grow dramatically. Clearly, the old mode of delivery involving paper and person-to-person contact at advising sites did not begin to meet the demand for information. Presumably, students are receiving more, timely, and better information and have a better opportunity to make better academic choices. The value of these services has increased for the student.

More problematic for the university is a more aggressive entry into and capture of a percentage of the distance education market. Timing will be critical and time is being lost to external vendors. Business plans are needed to determine demand, potential return on investment, and so forth. Open, nonproprietary, and extensible Internet protocols must be developed through organizations such as the Distributed Learning Network, sponsored by MHEC. Included here are object-oriented authoring tools, Internet communication protocols (e-mail, message management), and Internet collaboration protocols (chat, application sharing).

In the interim, higher education has not come to view Web-based distance education as a disruptive technology (Christensen,

1997). Current customers do not value it. The clients who are interested (adult knowledge workers) are not yet recognized as a sufficiently sized market to warrant investment. Faculty members are not prepared, nor are they interested in developing materials and teaching in this arena. There is an absence of enabling policies. The leadership is not committed, there is a lack of capital to support what is seen as a lower priority, and there is no plan to guide transformation.

The Internet offers many new possibilities—especially the building of learning communities that take advantage of new pedagogically sophisticated computer-mediated instructional materials and teaching techniques. Lectures and coursework can be organized and archived in a network. Materials, such as e-books, can be used and reused throughout the university and imported from other institutions. They are readily customizable and flexible and can be delivered live and synchronously over the network, or they can be delivered asynchronously anytime and anywhere. Already, Time Warner Trade Publishing, Alfred Knopf, Random House, and Simon & Schuster have announced that they will release e-books using Microsoft's new reader text-display software. Time Warner has indicated an interest in soliciting and publishing original manuscripts on-line through a Web site called IPublish.com, which is similar to Xlibris. Xlibris publishes books, secures ISBN numbers, and makes materials available for custom printing orders through Amazon.com.

Currently, our strategy is one of reaching niche markets, primarily by the professional schools. *Syndication* remains a foreign term in our vocabulary. Our delivery remains too faculty-centric, in my opinion, rather than learner-centric. The new audience of new-economy adult learners seeks convenient and flexible access to education and just-in-time delivery of information. They will want greater control over what is taught and when and how it is taught.

As long as the cost of delivery and development of instructional materials remains high, the market will be slow to develop. In the interim, we do not have an overall business plan or (syndication) strategy to address this market and its potential. Minimally, we need to maintain lifelong relationships through portals with our alumni by providing continuing education. In this way, we are able to maximize the yield on existing customer relationships.

Perfect Information

In the past, sellers did an enormous amount of customer research to determine the buyers' needs, preferences, and behaviors. Missing in the equation was the ability of customers to do similar research on the quality, price, and availability of goods and services. Customers were dependent upon advertising, a few consumer guidebooks, and word of mouth. This has totally changed with the browser and the Internet; now buyers can compete to the point of determining price. Customers have an enormous number of choices with the click of a mouse. And they are almost instantaneously able to compare both qualitative and quantitative data, which they can use to make a decision. Note: I am informed that several small private colleges have allowed students to bid on tuition.

The ramifications for the university are enormous, and an interesting example is the role of the admissions office. Traditionally, the admissions office has been the gatekeeper of information about a particular institution; now, students are routinely bypassing the office and going directly to faculty members and external sources of information via the Internet for information about programs of interest. More so than ever, it is critical that the admissions office use e-business to better understand the needs of students and customize their services and processes to attract them to the university. The ability to fully understand the preferences and priorities of students and their parents is mandatory. It is also the case that the admissions office will need to explore horizontal relationships with external vendors, as students can apply to multiple colleges via private on-line application services. In short, the admissions office will need to use e-business to create targeted, on-line marketing campaigns, manage customer relationships, and analyze site and application usage.

A similar argument can be made for the alumni office and institutional relations. The university, more so than many other organizations, has a complex set of constituencies that increasingly have and want more information about their university. Universities increasingly will need to find ways to respond to this demand.

Short Time Frame

Once upon a time, commerce depended upon the design of a product, means of production, marketing, planning, and sales personnel—all coordinated by a single entity and coming together in a physical place. This is not the case with e-business. Supply chains can be forged quickly through desktop computers, and the life cycle of many products is short.

University research, to a degree, has been distributed across institutions. It has been quick to adapt to the Internet. A greater challenge exists in the missions of teaching and outreach, especially when these services are provided at a distance. These remain vertically integrated activities and likely will need to adapt quickly to horizontal integration if they are to succeed. I believe we will see entertainment companies with strong capabilities in packaging and distributing content emerge as potential partners with universities, with faculty members providing content. This assumes that universities will develop the will and ability to build curricula much faster, especially in continuing education and lifelong learning. And they will need to create the curriculum together with their students and their students' employers. In the twenty-first century, more and more of our faculty members will primarily serve as designers of learning experiences, processes, and environments. The first indication of this trend is the emergence of commercial portals such as Blackboard and eCollege.

Note that these emerging partnerships will inevitably stress current contractual relationships with faculty members and their institutions. The faculty member who produces it currently owns his or her course material. As opportunities arise to sell these products to external vendors, universities will lose revenue and control of the learning process, especially as the outside vendors move upmarket from short courses and skills training to less expensive freshman courses that students will try to transfer to their home institution. Harvard University has already taken action against several of their faculty members who have moved into this market. A very critical question is, who owns a university course, as a course becomes more mobile in the Web environment?

Joint Creation of Goods and Services by Providers and Their Customers

Joint creation (or co-creation) is a collaboration of the customer and producer working together to create a product. The challenge for the company is to decide with the customer what value added is for both parties. The private sector provides interesting examples. In the area of buying, for example, Dell meets customer needs through customer customization of products that are built to order. And companies increasingly add value by providing software through downloading rather than by selling and mailing disks. The challenge is to find new ways to distribute goods and services at a cost considered reasonable by the customer. Interesting examples at the university include grants management and Web-based student services that were jointly built by administrators, students, and staff members. The real challenge will be in the substance, design, and delivery of education, especially for adult learners.

How Do We Proceed and Who Will Be Affected First?

E-business implementation proceeds in phases. Typically, units begin by using the Web to acquire or provide information on-line. Examples include description of policies and procedures and on-line catalogs and syllabi. The University of Minnesota has proceeded further in key service areas through the integration of internal services. Key examples are purchasing and procurement (Forms Nirvana) and one-stop student services. Purchasing, for example, goes from a paper process to an electronic paper process and then to a decision-support environment with opportunities to plan and assess performance as part of the buying decision. On-line university catalogs offer one-stop purchasing with the university's preferred vendors and goods, favorable pricing, and enforcement of purchasing policies (including more flexible spending limits for approved items), streamlined accounting, and monitoring of purchasing activity and inventory.

What awaits is the transformation and emergence of services that integrate outside organizations into our business strategy and processes. Partners, be they suppliers or customers, will increasingly be brought deeper into university processes and vice versa. This will require a much greater degree of openness and transparency on the part of the university than is currently the case. E-business benefits from speeding up and automating the university's own internal processes and also from spreading efficiency gains to the business systems of its suppliers and customers. We may need to both reengineer and reinvent much of what we do.

This has major implications for the university's enterprise system. Needed in the coming phase are electronic links that provide a seamless flow of information between an enterprise customer and its partners. Enterprise application integration is defined as the sharing of data in support of shared business processes among any connected applications or data sources. In its simplest form, integration can mean the ability to export data files from one application and import them into another application, possibly undergoing some translation between different data formats. More sophisticated forms will allow the partners to invoke actions in a target system. The current reluctance of units such as the registrar or financial aid to permit such participation results in much greater work for their customers—faculty members, admissions offices, advisors, and so forth.

Another example of the phased development of e-business is the design of the Web page or portal. The earliest pages at the University of Minnesota were organized by content or institutional organization. According to my colleague Carl Jacobsen of the University of Delaware, with this model the physical campus runaround becomes a runaround by mouse. Better strategies are portals organized by customer or context. For example, our student and staff one-stop portals are substantial improvements over earlier designs. They can be further narrowed by context—for example, students registering or parents visiting campus. But best yet is the customization of the page for each individual interacting with the university. At Minnesota, this is illustrated by One Stop—at Onestop.umn.edu. This portal is, in effect, an abridged version of the institutional Web site tailored to the individual, which can be added to, subtracted from, and modified at will. It gives each user a unique, personal, and preferred perspective of the university.

Portals, when used by all members of the university community as their desktop, will radically change how we do business. The units that are mostly likely to be affected first by portals and e-business are service units that function as intermediaries between a producer and a consumer of a good or service. It is probably the case that where you have the greatest risk you have the greatest opportunity. These units in particular must work with customers to find ways to provide value that customers are willing to pay for. And their costs must be factored into whatever solution we come up with. Units that currently provide intermediate services, such as the registrar or bookstores, need to rethink how they are organized, the service paradigm they employ, how they are funded, their division of labor, and the possibility of outsourcing cherished processes.

The bookstore provides an excellent example. The bookstore at the University of Minnesota is currently getting out of computer sales. They simply cannot compete in price, ready customization of products, and subsequent delivery, given the emergence of on-line sales and service. The next challenge is the sale and delivery of new and used textbooks. Already, textbook vendors are sending e-mails to students and faculty members, offering better prices to students and referral fees to faculty members. Auction sites are appearing for student-to-student sales of used books. American publishers are now assessing the demand for and delivery of e-books. How does the bookstore add value in this environment?

It can add some value by offering its own e-sale of books, which our bookstore has done. It can deliver quickly, which is important, as students tend to buy their books at the last moment and usually after they have completed any drops and additions of courses. And the bookstore can have a generous exchange policy for used books. But it can add major value if it partners with other university services and fully integrates its business processes. For example, on completion of on-line registration, the student is given a consolidated book order for his or her classes, which can be ordered and paid for through the student's university account in one stop as part of the registration process. Identifying these horizontal links and building integrated and Web-based processes is key to success throughout the university.

E-Business Service Models

E-business typically begins with units providing supplier-centric applications, which are essentially passive Web sites. Customers are provided with the ability to check on the availability of courses and view instructor as well as pricing (tuition and fees) information. More valuable to an organization and its clients are user-centric or self-service applications. These are often active or interactive Web sites that provide, for example, on-line account inquiry and maintenance, employee benefits management, purchasing and expense reporting, bill presentment and settlement, degree auditing, and so forth. Customers are allowed to securely view their account information, manage their accounts, analyze information, and initiate transactions on a 24x7 basis.

Many of the e-business models in use are business transplants. Amazon.com, for example, uses a Web site as a storefront to sell physical goods that are delivered by a third party. Business-to-customer models like this are likely to be adopted by a number of university units engaged in external sales. Libraries can use this approach to deliver or renew books. Another example is a sell-side e-business that addresses marketing and sales and handles order management fulfillment. Included here are catalogs, configurators, shopping carts, order management, and payment. University auxiliaries are most likely to adapt this business model. Also under development are buy-side business-to-business applications that are used by organizations to manage their purchasing.

Another recent development of a business-to-business application is the advertising-based e-business. Here, third-party fees support the operation of a free service. The alumni association and athletics have been approached by an e-business business that develops specialized portals for free. Both parties share in advertising and sales revenues that are generated by clients using the portal. Subscription-based Web sites are a variant that has application at the university as well.

Of great interest are new business models that are made possible or necessary by the Internet. Especially noteworthy are e-business models based on auctions, which are of various types, such as Yankee, Dutch, and reverse auctions. The reverse auction is of particular interest to the university. Here, a consumer-to-business model is used, which permits buyers to post a price they are willing to pay for an item, and the site then facilitates a match with a seller—for example, Priceline.com. Used textbook sales (a consumer-to-consumer e-business model) may ultimately be relegated to such auction sites, which probably ought to be developed by the university in cooperation with the bookstores. Related sites could be developed for classified ads, as is the case at the University of Delaware.

Noteworthy, too, is software to manage constituency relationships. For example, constituency e-mail management applications are now available to facilitate all phases of the communication between units and their clients. The programs have the ability to route incoming e-mail messages to appropriate destinations. Another feature is audited call director functionality, where a workflow mechanism is used for moving incoming messages through a series of steps necessary to generate a response. The programs employ knowledge- or rule-based systems capable of creating or suggesting an appropriate response to each message. Case management systems allow incoming e-mail messages that are continuations of previous interactions to be associated with the history of that interaction. No less important are sophisticated tracking and trend analysis capabilities that further enhance management of customer relationships.

The capacity to exploit a rich body of data is what makes these systems potentially powerful for the university. In addition to transactional data, information can be collected on who visits Web sites and with what frequency and for how long, as well as what banners they hit. This supports one-to-one marketing and the ability to better respond to customer preferences. There are enormous policy ramifications here, which will be discussed later in this chapter.

Many university units, such as admissions, the alumni associations, institutional relations, and the foundations, will use such systems. Rather than reinvent the wheel dozens of times throughout the institution, a central strategy would be very useful here.

Last, and perhaps most interesting, is the emergence of "infomediaries," a word coined by John Hagel of McKinsey. Infomediaries sell information about a market and create a platform on which buyers and sellers can do business. In so doing, they add value as intermediaries between suppliers and their customers. Key, here, is the willingness of the customer to pay for the added value. An example is Chemdex, which is an aggregator of multiple vendor catalogs into a single, searchable Web-accessible database. Buyers in fragmented markets can select products at up-to-the-minute prices and get product information in a single contact point for service.

Chemdex markets research chemicals to universities and pharma-
ceutical companies. Pricing becomes far more competitive as the
customer effectively buys at an auction or commodity price of the day
(Kaplan and Sawhney, 2000).

This development has enormous ramifications for university
stores as well as for how purchasing sets up business systems to take
full advantage of newly created auction markets for goods needed
by the university community. Some of our intermediary businesses,
like the financial aid office, may survive by becoming infomediaries, in the sense that they rationalize and aggregate previously
unstructured encounters between them and their customers. For
example, greater emphasis may be placed on capturing customer
information and developing detailed profiles of an individual's need
requirements.

Rebuilding Value or Supply Chains in Education

E-business is premised upon finding ways of adding value to established and linked business processes. By analogy, e-business in education will focus on finding value in the teaching process, which
includes curriculum development (programming), content development (production), learner delivery (delivery), learner acquisition, assessment, articulation, and credentialing. These links can
be pulled apart, becoming a virtual value chain that is nonlinear, a
matrix of potential inputs and outputs that can be accessed and distributed through a wide variety of channels.

Other higher education value chains involve service areas and
include marketing (providing information to prospective students),
admissions (qualifying and selecting students), enrollment services
(registration, billing, and financial aid), academic support (advising and tutoring), student services (placement, counseling, and information technology help), and credentialing (grades, degrees,
certificates, and transcripts). The University of Minnesota has come
a long way in this area with the development of on-line registration

systems, advising portfolios, and one-stop portals where transactions, planning, performance assessment, and marketing functions have been developed.

The consequences for higher education are huge, as hundreds of new companies, each specializing in one link of the value chain, can and will emerge. These companies may supply products and services to institutions or they may decide to bypass them and go directly to students. An example is SMARTHINKING, which is an Internet company that provides human, real-time, on-line academic support at any time of day for core courses in higher education.

Students can feel overwhelmed by the flood of information available to them through the Internet and the university libraries' large collection of on-line and print resources. Research Quickstart and Quickstudy are two Web-based tools designed to make research more manageable and effective for undergraduate students.

Research QuickStart (http://research.lib.umn.edu) is a wizard-like tool that generates dynamic Web pages for over two hundred subjects. Students can use Research Quickstart to access a selective list of subject resources chosen by librarians who are information experts in their discipline. Quickstart subject pages contain links to on-line subscription databases and Web sites, as well as listings of print resources when appropriate.

QuickStudy (http://tutorial.lib.umn.edu) is a Web-based tutorial that teaches students information literacy skills necessary for research in the University of Minnesota libraries and on the Web. QuickStudy's eight modules contain lessons on a variety of topics, including designing a research strategy, conducting an effective keyword search, evaluating Web sites, and citing sources. QuickStudy lessons also contain exercises and quizzes to help students practice what they have learned.

Portfolio is a powerful advising tool that allows students to incorporate a rich array of their collective work and life experiences into a site that can be shared with advisers, employers, and others with whom the student wants to share information.

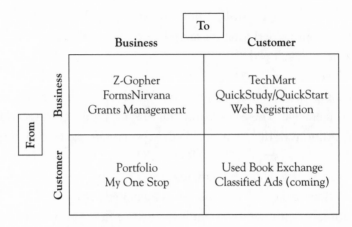

Figure 5.1. E-Business Models

Trends and Issues

Delivery of Education and Conduct of Research

The new information technologies associated with portals and e-business are likely to have a profound impact on how higher education's mission is delivered. In particular:

- Information technology will present the possibility of greater customization of courses and programs, combined with enhanced flexibility of delivery.

- The communication of research is likely to be more varied, with formal publication playing a less significant role, while the current improvements in access to research findings and library collections are likely to accelerate.

- To stay competitive in the new environment, knowledge workers have to stay current. As a result, lifelong learning will be the dominant paradigm for higher education in the twenty-first century. Information technology is driving an increasing emphasis on establishing and maintaining effective learning relationships with students throughout their lives. The knowledge age requires constant, individualized learning, and information technology supports such learning.

- The Internet is associated with interaction, unlike television, which is associated with passivity. As a result, the Internet becomes a far more interesting tool for distance education. Not only can students receive information, they can also practice the application of that information in the context of previous knowledge. The Internet provides much more than two-way video and voice communication. It allows authenticated and confidential submission of homework assignments and even tests, the ability to replay lessons or information on a 24x7 basis, and the ability to collaborate remotely with other students on projects.

Service Issues

The technologies under discussion will also influence how institutional services are organized and delivered and the very strategies around which institutional services are developed.

- University service units will become more client-focused and seamless. The new enterprise systems and organization are designed to provide students, faculty members, and staff members with greater quantity and quality, as well as timely accessibility to data that is integrated and supports institutional and personnel strategic planning and decision making. Service units will help build and support an environment in which their clients are provided knowledge and know-how to apply information to a given problem. Central administrators will drive decision making down into the organization with minimal intervention.

- Services will be provided electronically rather than in a paper mode and without intermediation by the staff. Services will be increasingly accessible at any time from any place. Intermediary services become less relevant as students, faculty members, and staff members are able to have direct contact with the producers of services.

- Value-added activities such as planning, performance assessment, and marketing play an ever-increasing role in the design of systems and services that replace improvements in transaction processes and efficiency as the primary drivers for change.

Risk and Conflict Management Issues

E-business is raising a number of new policy questions that need to be addressed in the future. In some areas, such as libel and defamation, it may simply be a matter of modifying existing policy to accommodate the digital environment. Other areas, such as copyright, patent, and trademark infringements (intellectual property) and privacy, are more problematic. The unprecedented ability of institutions to acquire personal information, to combine this information in unique ways, and to store massive amounts of this information will raise significant privacy and security issues. What responsibilities do we have as an institution to safeguard the information we capture about our community? What are our responsibilities under the Family Educational Rights and Privacy Act of 1974 (FERPA)? Are we protecting faculty and institutional intellectual properties? What policies and regulations are needed in the handling of digital data and information? Areas that need to be addressed include

- Academic policies on credentials and accepting of credits for on-line courses

- Self certification (by the client)

- Authentication processes (security, digital signatures, unauthorized access)

- Greater access to data (privacy) and user rights and responsibilities

- Policies on data administration and management and management of licensed software information resources

- Neglected sites that make inaccurate, anachronistic, and obsolete information available to outsiders

- Denial of access or repudiation of service (resource usage—for example, Napster) and acceptable use and user responsibilities

- Copyright, patent, and trademark infringements (intellectual property)

- Commercial use of campus resources and electronic payments

- Advertising

- Defamation

- Legal and regulatory issues (taxes and tariffs, regulated products, freedom of speech, illegal activities)

- Local decision making and accountability

- Americans with Disabilities Act (ADA) compliance

Universities currently have many certification requirements that are cumbersome and incongruent with the concept of student empowerment. Do students need to be "certified" to take courses through as many prerequisite course requirements as there exist today? Research at the University of Minnesota has indicated that students who self-select courses regardless of prerequisites perform in those courses as well as or better than students who had met the requirements.

Data Administration and Management

How are the data going to be shared, and who should have access to what data? What institutional record policies are needed, especially with regard to who owns what information? What are the official data when units develop "shadow" systems and institutional databases are not integrated? Such a situation makes it very difficult to manage information in a way that ensures its accuracy and integrity.

Authentication

Increasingly, in a networked environment, institutions will need to have ways to authenticate that people accessing particular data are who they say they are. This is related to the challenge of establishing a system that can authorize an individual for access to particular data. Such authentication and authorization systems depend on having information policies in place that address who can access what data.

User Rights and Responsibilities

Policies regarding user rights and responsibilities, including commercial use of campus resources, are necessary. Also, resource usage must be addressed. Recent episodes involving the use of Napster have demonstrated the need for students to understand their need to use the resources responsibly. Users have not only rights but also responsibilities in the networked information environment. And colleges and universities should ensure that students are educated about these rights and responsibilities.

Academic Policies

Credentialing standards need to be adopted that support and promote high-quality e-learning in our institutions. Current practices are generally strict and there is a tendency not to accept credits from other institutions, especially for on-line courses. In an e-learning environment, campuses will have to revisit these kinds of policies. The university will need a comprehensive policy that addresses this and other barriers that current policies present to e-learning.

Advertising and Revenue Distribution

Although some institutions have policy in this area, there are more issues in a networked environment than there have been in the past. There are many opportunities arising to generate new revenues from advertising on Web sites. One of the greatest problems has to do with subunits on campus contracting with vendors on their own, in the absence of institutional policy addressing the specifics of Web advertising. There are also sponsorships possible in this new environment that institutions need to consider and manage. This raises an issue as to where the revenues should go from such sponsorships and contracts. Click-through revenues are on the increase, and this was seen as a possible source of revenue for institutions, but there is a need to manage this practice, as well. These issues prompt the need for policy in this area.

Pricing Policies

With e-learning on the rise, institutions will need to reexamine their pricing policies, especially to enable market-based pricing and to accommodate out-of-state or international students as e-learning allows more distant participation. (See Shapiro and Varian, 1999, on the economics of information and differential pricing.)

Organizational Issues

- Organizational structures do not align with functions (such as e-business and classrooms).

- Organizations must be flatter, less hierarchical, and broader in function, with greater control of resources in order to support the new service environment. There is a shift in power and control in the new environment.

Personnel Issues

- Within the next decade, new jobs at the university will increasingly require analytic ability, creativity, and familiarity with new technologies.

- Flexibility in jobs and the need for generalists will require broad banding of jobs.

- Automation, paperless transactions, and one-stop self-service shifts greater responsibility and participation in administrative services to the customer, and this changes the need for labor as well as the division of labor within the organization.

- Student services, HR, and grants management professionals will become generalists serving as facilitators and navigators in an information-rich environment that is shared by provider and client alike.

Note

1. E-business is defined herein as the transformation of key business processes through the use of Internet technologies. E-commerce refers to trade transactions carried on by buyers and sellers over the Web.

References

Blustain, H., Goldstein, P., and Lozier, G. "Assessing the New Competitive Landscape." In R. N. Katz. *Dancing with the Devil*. San Francisco: Jossey-Bass, 1998.

Christensen, C. M. *The Innovator's Dilemma: When New Technologies Cause Great Firms to Fail*. Boston: Harvard Business School Press, 1997.

Kaplan S., and Sawhney, M. "E-Hubs: The New B2B Marketplaces." *Harvard Business Review*, May-June 2000, pp. 97–103.

Puryear, R., and Melnicoff, R. M. "The eEconomy: It's Later Than You Think."
    Outlook, 1999, *2*, 33–43.

Shapiro, C., and Varian, H. *Information Rules: A Strategic Guide to the Network
    Economy*. Boston, Mass.: Harvard Business School Press, 1999.

Shrivastava, P. "Management Classes as Online Learning Communities." *Journal
    of Management Education*, 1999, *23*(6).

Werbach, K. "Syndication: The Emerging Model for Business in the Internet
    Era." *Harvard Business Review*, May-June 2000, pp. 85–93.

6

The Business Challenges

Diana Oblinger and Larry Goldstein

You don't have to be in business (or even be a net-generation company) to be influenced by e-business. E-business has created new alternatives for individuals and institutions, offering them more options than ever before in terms of convenience, selection, and cost. Even traditional institutions are being affected. Just as these born-on-the-Web companies signal new ways of thinking about business, the patterns of e-business are shifting expectations in education. Those expectations can range from instantaneous access to convenience to cost competitiveness. Opportunities for economies of scale and enhanced "customer" experiences will have an impact on education, as well.

Beyond university business processes that may align well with traditional businesses, there are e-business principles that have the potential to affect the core of the institution. Dozens of net-generation companies have become part of the educational landscape (see Table 6.1).

This chapter explores e-business trends that may have an impact on traditional higher education institutions.

Operating Efficiencies

Many of the first e-business applications in higher education will likely be aimed at improving operating efficiencies. Because educational

Table 6.1. Examples of E-Business Vendors in Education

Process Area	Some of the E-Business Vendors
On-line admissions applications	Embark, CollegeNet, XAP
On-line student services	Campus Pipeline, YouthStream's MyBytes.com, Jenzabar.com
On-line procurement	CommerceOne, Ariba
On-line alumni communities, contributions, and merchandising	Harris Publishing, Alumniconnections.com
On-line course delivery	Blackboard, Centra, Convene, eCollege.com, WebCT
On-line content distributors	Caliber, UNext.com, Pensare
Learning portals	Click2learn.com, Hungry Minds, Ziff-Davis, SmartPlanet.com, Blackboard.com

Source: Kidwell, Mattie, and Sousa, 2000. Used by permission.

institutions strive to keep costs low so that education is more afford-able for learners, e-business may become a vitally important tool. Educational institutions are beginning to capitalize on improved operating efficiencies by eliminating paper transactions and reengi-neering processes, and using the Web for "comparison shopping."

E-business can systematically reduce transaction costs. By squeez-ing time and distance out of the equation, e-business can eliminate many of the costs that we have long assumed to be more or less fixed (Hartman, Sifonis, and Kador, 2000). In higher education we tend to assume that we must shoulder the costs associated with purchase orders, manually transmitted forms, multiple signatures, and a well-established bureaucracy. E-business is causing us to challenge those assumptions.

Eliminating Paper with E-Procurement

Virtually any organization can generate savings by capitalizing on less expensive ways of processing transactions. Conceptually, this is relatively simple. By eliminating the need to receive forms and invoices in paper format and then manually rekeying them into applications, organizations can reduce costs. A traditional paper bill costs about ninety cents in postage and processing, according to industry estimates. On-line services can cut that cost by thirty to fifty cents per bill (PricewaterhouseCoopers, 1998).

E-procurement can be thought of as using digital technology for paperless procurement. This may involve electronic data interchange (EDI), digital processing of transactions, order management, inventory control, or the use of on-line, dynamic pricing. The move to e-procurement is often motivated by the desire to reduce cycle time, ensure faster processing, and reduce error rates.

Estimates are that a traditional purchase requisition costs $150 to process. With e-procurement the costs range from $10 to $15. Additional efficiencies and price discounts may lead to an additional 10 percent in savings (for example, finding goods and services at a lower price). HigherMarkets and CommonFind are firms that create e-procurement systems for educational institutions. The systems allow institutions to do on-line procurement and to aggregate purchases across multiple institutions.

State agencies are seeing big benefits from on-line procurement. Last year the state of Pennsylvania bought 155,000 tons of anthracite coal through Internet auctions. It paid $10 million, which was $1 million less than it expected to spend. The state also bought 972,000 tons of road salt for $30 million through a Web auction, a savings of $2.5 million (Birnbaum, 2000).

Requests for Proposals (RFPs) are another area that may be transformed by e-procurement. An example is provided by DABS—Defense Automated Bidders Service. The bidding process is a time-consuming, inefficient process, involving cumbersome paperwork. Realizing the efficiencies gained via the Internet, organizations are now starting to move these RFP processes on-line. DABS, being tested by Baruch Defense Marketing, is a first move by the government to automate the RFP process. By using dynamic pricing via the Internet, the government can save time, money, and labor resources that can be used elsewhere (Open Site, 1999).

Reducing the Cost of Service Delivery

The Web and e-business principles are allowing institutions to reduce the cost of service delivery. Perhaps more than other entities, educational institutions must contain the cost of service delivery—in part because of the desire to keep costs down, but also because so much of what occurs in educational institutions is related to the delivery of a service (for example, student services, human resources, and library resources).

Some services, such as admissions, are based on paper applications processed by the staff. West Virginia Wesleyan College (WVWC) has partnered with Embark to move to an entirely electronic application process. Establishing the process will cost WVWC $25,000 for the first year and $15,000 for each subsequent year. WVWC will also pay Embark a $10 fee per application; applicants pay WVWC a $30 fee. The college expects to save money. Under the old system, printing costs alone exceeded $30,000. In addition, the admitted student typically received thirty-four pieces of mail, from initial inquiry to acceptance. Switching to e-mail will eliminate production and postage costs. The new software is expected to relieve the staff of mundane chores such as data entry, as well (University Business, 2000).

Across a host of segments (such as retail and banking), alternative mechanisms for providing customer service are being used. In business, for example, respective figures for the cost of service are

- Direct sales force: $250 to $400 per customer contact
- Telecoverage: $30 to $40 per customer contact

- Telemarketing: $3 to $8 per customer contact

- Direct mail: $1 to $4 per customer contact

- World Wide Web: $0.01 to $0.50 per customer contact (Greene, 2000)

Although these functions do not coincide with higher education processes, they do illustrate the order-of-magnitude difference between face-to-face delivery and on-line access.

In the last few years we have seen many examples of services being delivered over the Web rather than face-to-face. At the University of Minnesota it was found that this better met student expectations and allowed the institution to concentrate its personnel in areas where students most needed personal attention.

For example, the number of transactions managed by student service units is enormous. Hundred of thousands of grades are reported and recorded, thousands of students are registered, and several hundred million dollars of tuition and fees are collected. Many of these transactions are done manually, on paper, at fixed times and at fixed locations.

Fully 75 to 90 percent of all transactions currently done manually and on paper should be done electronically and without the intervention of an administrator. Moreover, these transactions should be linked strategically to minimize runaround. For example, dropping a course should automatically and simultaneously adjust financial aid, credit a student's account, and notify a student of the academic or financial consequences of his or her decision (Kvavik and Handberg, 1999).

The University of Minnesota student Web site receives in excess of thirteen million hits a month, and three million pages of information are downloaded. The numbers continue to grow dramatically. Clearly the old mode of delivery involving paper and person-to-person contact at advising sites did not begin to meet the demand for information. Presumably students are receiving more, timely, and better information and have a better opportunity to make better academic choices. As Kvavik indicates, the value of these services has increased for the student.

When discussing on-line versus in-person services, two points should be made. First, there is an up-front cost to developing the infrastructure needed to move from a face-to-face delivery mode to one that is Web-based. Such transitions are neither inexpensive nor easy. However, they are possible. Examples can be found at the University of Minnesota, Deakin University (Australia), and West Virginia Wesleyan College.

Second, this chapter does not advocate the delivery of all services via the Web—perhaps not even the majority. However, if there are ways to conserve resources by delivering services in a different mode (for example, over the Web), then the institution has the opportunity to reinvest those resources in other high-priority areas, such as teaching and learning. In many discussions we continue to hear the argument that the delivery of services via the Web is impersonal. When we ask students, we find that most of them prefer the accessibility and flexibility of Web-based systems to many face-to-face situations (Robert Kvavik, personal communication, May 2000).

Infomediaries

E-business can also reduce the costs of service delivery by lowering transaction and search costs. This often occurs by aggregating and providing information about sellers, customers, and prospects. A common term for these aggregators is infomediary.

Infomediaries bring together buyers and sellers and provide value by offering advice, service, or other benefits. Infomediaries can serve as aggregators of prospects or as buyer advocates. Although infomediaries typically own nothing, they sell information about a market and create a platform on which buyers and sellers can do business.

A business world example is Autobytel.com. Their goal is to make car buying and selling as painless as possible. To do that,

Autobytel.com aggregates information about car buyers and, on behalf of its car dealer partners, wraps a streamlined set of services around the whole process. Autobytel.com enables dealers to sell more cars while reducing marketing costs. Typically, car dealers have to pay marketing costs that average $335 per car sold. By becoming a member of the Autobytel.com network, a dealer's marketing costs drop to an average of $86 per car. The reduced costs benefit the consumer, as well as the dealer (Hartman, Sifonis and Kador, 2000).

Contentville.com is an education-oriented infomediary. The site sells books, dissertations, and legal documents and provides other material of interest to academics, such as literary advice columns. Contentville will sell any book in print through an arrangement with Ingram Book Group. The site emphasizes journal articles, magazines, scholarly research, transcripts, and historical documents. Contentville has relationships with a number of providers, including EBSCO and Primedia for magazine and journal subscriptions, Bell & Howell for dissertations, and Libris for rare books. They will also sell electronic books. Contentville will make its money by marketing and selling the products of others. As part of its marketing services the site features recommendations from a roster of contributing editors. The site also carries advice to readers (Blumenstyk, 2000).

Although we commonly talk about the network causing disintermediation of traditional functions, the pattern of infomediaries is the opposite: they aggregate information and services. At this point in the evolution of e-business, infomediaries generate the lion's share of value in the network economy and will continue to do so for the foreseeable future. The infomediary model has proven to be a reliable source of generating new wealth. Infomediaries range from portals such as Yahoo! to net start-ups that are creating unique markets on the net (Hartman, Sifonis and Kador, 2000).

Hungrymindsuniversity.com operates as an on-line learning portal that aggregates courseware from academic institutions and corporate training providers. They currently advertise over seventeen thousand on-line learning experiences. Their key academic partners include the University of California at Berkeley, UCLA Extension, the University of Maryland, New York University, and the University of Phoenix.

MindEdge.com has created a large, searchable database of on-line courses. They intend to expand their offerings to include services such as enrollment, billing, and marketing (Carr and Blumenstyk, 2000).

Another aggregator, Smart Force, is focused on the training, rather than the education, market. Smart Force provides an integrated learning environment—everything from career planning to Internet-delivered courses, instructor-led workshops, and mentoring. Their clients include corporations and government agencies, such as Unisys, Cisco, Compaq, the U.S. Army, the U.S. Postal Service, and the U.S. Internal Revenue Service.

Headlight.com is an aggregator of up-to-date training designed for the computer and the Internet. They tailor courses to an individual learner's abilities by matching the learner's profile to class content learning objectives. Learners are able to concentrate on areas where they need extra practice. Their key content partners include DigitalThink, Skillsoft, and ElementK.

At the moment, most infomediaries are focused on goods and services rather than courses. For example, edu.com is one of many companies competing for the student e-commerce market. The firm provides deep-discount brand-name products for college students. Edu.com sells computers, software, bank services, phone and Internet services, textbooks, credit cards, and electronics (*Virtual University News*, 2000c). CollegeClub is a Web site that markets a variety of academic and recreational services to students. Specifically designed to cater to the eighteen- to twenty-four-year-old, CollegeClub relies on advertising, shopping, and "bounties" (flat fees for signing up users for credit cards, and so forth) (Looney, 2000). Final-exam.com offers on-line study guides for students in survey courses. PinkMonkey.com offers literature summaries, links to academic resources for research, and reference, as well as SAT preparation and college planning.

Price Comparisons

On-line users—whether individuals or institutions—are finding the Internet a perfect place to compare prices. Shopping for compact discs, for instance, a consumer can expect to visit about three bricks-and-mortar stores in one hour. In the on-line world, using a shopping agent, a consumer can reach about fifty suppliers in an hour or get exposure to five hundred suppliers in the same time frame. Even big-ticket items are not immune from this new market transparency. In 1998, a quarter of U.S. automobile purchasers used the Internet for research before buying. By the year 2000, nearly 50 percent of U.S. car buyers used the Internet for research before buying. In fact, product research already is the third most common on-line activity in the United States (IBM, 1999).

Search costs are practically nil for individuals with access to the Web. For certain kinds of commodity or standardized goods, the buyer has close to, if not absolutely, perfect information about the material facts of the market beforehand. Often, it would cost next to nothing for the buyer to switch his or her purchasing from one seller to another (for example, for textbooks, chemical supplies, or office supplies). Negligible search costs, perfect information, and low switching costs were simply unheard of before the Web. Today it is becoming almost routine (Rappa, 2000c).

Potential comparisons go well beyond price. In the past it was difficult for individuals to research the quality, price, and availability of goods and services. They were dependent upon advertising, a few consumer guidebooks, and word of mouth. This has totally changed with the ability to browse on the Internet, to the point where buyers can set their own price for some goods and services. Individuals can almost instantaneously compare both qualitative and quantitative data, which they can use to make a decision.

The technology that enables one to assess the market and find the best price is an intelligent agent, also called a "shopping bot." A shopping bot is a software program that runs autonomously, or semi-autonomously, and carries out user directives continuously. The agent can be personalized to the user, and preferences can be programmed *a priori* or learned in use over time. Already, dozens of specialized shopping bots are available and many more are under development. Something less obvious, but equally important to remember, is that selling bots will also become an increasingly common method by which sellers can come to understand consumer trends, as well as understand the competition (Rappa, 2000d).

There are many situations in which comparison shopping might benefit education. For individual students, being able to shop for the lowest-price textbooks (including used ones) over the Web might save a significant amount of money. For the institution as a whole, cost savings could result from comparison shopping for many goods and services, such as IT components, office supplies, chemical supplies, and utilities.

Students already use the Internet to compare features and costs associated with higher education institutions. A recent survey of ten thousand U.S. high school students revealed that an institution's Web site is the third most important source of information for prospective students (Washington Post, Mar. 28, 2000).

The National Center for Education Statistics in the U.S. Department of Education has unveiled a Web site that lets students and parents comb through data on thousands of colleges and universities so that they can comparison shop when choosing where to go to college. IPEDS College Opportunities On-Line (COOL) contains information (such as cost of tuition, books and supplies, and housing) from thousands of public and private two- and four-year colleges and universities, as well as career schools. Statistics are available on degrees awarded, enrollment, student demographics, and the availability of financial aid (Carnevale, 2000).

Smaller-scale comparisons are possible, as well. The Ohio Learning Network is a consortium of public and independent colleges and universities. It recently launched a statewide catalog of distance education courses (OhioLEARNS!) that will allow potential students to make comparisons among over five hundred courses. The site also contains links for further information, enrollment, and textbook orders. Prospective students can also access distance learning specialists at host campuses across Ohio, who can answer questions, locate appropriate courses and degree programs, and provide "high touch" support (*Virtual University News*, 2000b).

Revenue Strategies

E-Pricing Models

Traditionally, higher education institutions—whether a residential campus or an adult education unit—have offered services for a fixed price. (Although many institutions "discount" tuition, there is a standard fixed price as the baseline.) Learners pay for courses based on rates determined by measures such as student credit hours. Spurred by alternatives piloted in e-business, the fixed price model may change for some. We have already seen U.S. institutions auction tuition and scholarships over the Internet.

With all the new business models, there is uncertainty over which to choose for what component of the educational enterprise. E-learning start-ups (and some educational institutions) are currently using a variety of models. A description of some revenue alternatives appears in Table 6.2.

Some models, such as seat licenses, subscription, and pay-for-use, are familiar to us, based on our experience with software or library resources. Others—such as dynamic pricing—offer a greater conceptual challenge to see their application in higher education.

Table 6.2. E-Business Revenue Alternatives

Pricing Model	Description
Dynamic pricing	The use of an auction to establish price
Advertising	The sale of advertising space on a Web site
Seat license	The licensing of content or software on a per-user basis (for example, license an entire library of courseware)
Subscription	The sale of e-learning services as a periodic payment
Pay for use	The sale of specific e-learning products and services (for example, purchase a specific course title)
Direct marketing/data collection	The sale of customer lists and market data

Source: Adapted from Peterson, Marostica, and Callahan, 1999.

Auctions

In e-business, auctioning is a popular pricing model. Rather than buying a good at a fixed price, nearly half of today's e-commerce is based on dynamic pricing, which is used in various types of auctions, such as open-cry auctions, Dutch auctions, and reverse auctions.

In an open-cry auction, also called an English auction, the buyers gather at a common location—physical or virtual—at a pre-specified time. Each buyer can hear or see the bid submitted by a rival buyer and has a limited time to respond to it with a higher counteroffer. In physical auctions, the responses must be received within seconds; in cyber-auctions, several minutes or hours may lapse (Kumar and Feldman, 2000).

In a Dutch auction, the auctioneer starts with a high asking price. The asking price is gradually decreased until buyers emerge with bids, specifying how many items they will purchase at the current asking price. The auctioneer can continue lowering the bid to maintain a stream of buyers while the inventory lasts (Kumar and Feldman, 2000).

In reverse auctions, also called name-your-price auctions, the prospective buyer makes a final (and usually binding) bid for a specified good or service. The broker's fee is then spread between the bid and fulfillment prices, perhaps with a processing charge, as well (Rappa, 2000b).

The reverse auction is of particular interest to educational institutions. Here, a consumer-to-business model is used that permits buyers to post a price they are willing to pay for an item, and the site then facilitates a match with a seller. A well-known example is Priceline.com. Used textbook sales (a consumer-to-consumer e-business model) may ultimately be relegated to such auction sites. Related sites could be developed for classified ads, as is the case at the University of Delaware.

As institutions strive to keep costs down, they may find that using auctions to procure goods and services saves money. The state of North Carolina is currently experimenting with selling excess property (such as surplus automobiles and furniture) via auctioning (Rick Webb, personal communication, June 2000). Many colleges and universities routinely sell surplus goods. On-line auctions may be as viable for higher education as they are for state government.

Dynamic pricing is also used in the government. The Commonwealth of Pennsylvania has adopted this concept. FreeMarkets.com is a company that creates on-line auctions so that sellers can compete for a buyer's business. Working with the state of Pennsylvania, FreeMarkets has saved $10 million on a procurement volume of $98 million through nine on-line auctions. The items involved in the auctions ranged from construction to telecommunications to license plates.

Other institutions may be intrigued by auctioning excess course capacity on the Internet. For example, Georgetown University announced that it would auction three seats in its multimedia immersion certification course on the Web. Whereas the normal tuition for the fifteen-week course is $10,000 bidders hoped to attend at discounted rates (*Virtual University News*, 2000a).

Advertising

A slightly more controversial and perhaps short-lived revenue strategy involves advertising. Funding the development of the e-learning infrastructure and on-line courses is a challenge. Many educational institutions and some government agencies are accepting the compromise of advertising in order to subsidize Web hosting and delivery.

There is already evidence of this trend in higher education. Many campuses in the United States are making agreements with firms like Campus Pipeline, where advertising was initially the primary source of revenue. In return, the build-out of the campus Web site and hosting services is provided at no charge. Campus Pipeline has since its inception reduced its dependence on advertising revenue.

Beyond Web sites, the next wave in Internet marketing may be "eduCommerce," a concept that combines on-line course offerings with advertising content. Several companies devoted to eduCommerce already exist, including Powered (formerly NotHarvard.com), Learn2.com, Smart Planet, and Hungry Minds. Some believe that eduCommerce may be viable as long as companies are careful with the amount and type of advertising. For example, Smart Planet permits advertisements on introductory pages but prohibits them within course pages (Oblinger, 2001).

Although it is unlikely that eduCommerce courses will ever dominate the on-line education market, many colleges and universities face stiff competition from newcomers that offer their courses for free. These entities count on sales generated from advertisements to make their profits and draw new learners (Guernsey, 2000).

Other Models

There are other business models employed in the commercial sector that are not common in education. However, as the number of new education ventures increases, some may adopt these models.

A *specialized portal* (or *vortal*—that is, vertical portal) is a site that attracts a well-defined user audience. Numbers are not as important as the homogeneity of the audience. For example, a site that attracts only golfers or home buyers or new parents can be highly sought after as a venue for certain advertisers who are willing to pay a premium to reach that particular audience. Predictions are that specialized portals will proliferate in the near future (Rappa, 2000b). There is likely to be a growing number of portals aimed at specific higher education audiences, such as graduating seniors.

There is a *pay-for-attention* model. In this case the site pays visitors for viewing content and completing forms, and it uses sweepstakes or frequent flyer-type point schemes. The attention marketing approach has the most appeal to companies with very complex product messages, which might otherwise find it hard to sustain customer interest. The approach was pioneered by CyberGold. To facilitate transactions, the company developed and patented a micropayment system (Rappa, 2000b).

Bargain discounters sell goods at or below cost. They seek to make a profit through advertising. An example is Buy.com (Rappa, 2000b).

A *recommender system* is a site that allows users to exchange information with one another about the quality of products and services—or the sellers with whom they have had a purchase experience (good or bad) (Rappa, 2000b).

The *affiliate model* provides purchasing opportunities wherever people may be surfing. This is in contrast with the generalized portal, which seeks to drive a high volume of traffic to one site. Affiliates operate by providing financial incentives to affiliated partner sites. The affiliate provides purchase-point click-through to the merchant. It is a pay-for-performance model—if the affiliate does not generate sales, it represents no cost to the merchant (Rappa, 2000b).

Conclusion

E-business offers higher education a variety of opportunities to eliminate paper, reduce the cost of service delivery, and compare prices. Educational institutions are beginning to adopt e-business principles to keep costs as low as possible so that education remains affordable.

At the same time that e-business is allowing institutions to contain costs, it is opening new opportunities for infomediaries in areas that range from precollege to postgraduation and from academic to administrative. While e-business is presenting us with multiple opportunities, it is also challenging our ability to rationalize auctions, advertising, and eduCommerce with our conventional practices.

References

Birnbaum, J. "Death to Bureaucrats, Good News for the Rest of Us." *Fortune*. June 26, 2000, pp. 241–244.

Blumenstyk, G. "Web Site Dispenses Books, Journals, Dissertations—and Literary Advice." *Chronicle of Higher Education*, July 6, 2000. [http://chronicle.com/free/2000/07/2000070601t.htm].

Carnevale, D. "Web Site Provides Detailed Information on U.S. Colleges." *The Chronicle of Higher Education*, Mar. 27, 2000.

Carr, S., and Blumenstyk, G. "The Bubble Bursts for Education Dot-coms." *The Chronicle of Higher Education*, June 30, 2000. [http://chronicle.com/free/v46/i43/43a03901.htm].

Greene, M. *E-business 2.0*. Mar. 7, 2000. Unpublished.

Guernsey, L. "Education: Web's New Come-On." *New York Times*, Mar. 16, 2000.

Hartman, A., Sifonis, J., and Kador, J. *Net Ready: Strategies for Success in the E-conomy*. New York: McGraw-Hill, 2000.

International Business Machines (IBM). *Global Market Trends*. 1999. Unpublished.

Kidwell, J., Mattie, J., and Sousa, M. "Prepare Your Campus for E-business." *EDUCAUSE Quarterly*, 2000, 23(2), 20–29.

Kumar, M., and Feldman, S. *Internet Auctions*, [http://www.ibm.com/iac/papers/auction_fp.pdf]. 2000.

Kvavik, R., and Handberg, M. "Transforming Student Services." In D. Oblinger and R. Katz (eds.), *Renewing Administration*. Bolton, Mass.: Anker Publishing, 1999.

Looney, M. "Virtual Campus Communities: A Potential Role for Portals." NLII Annual Meeting, New Orleans, La., Jan. 2000.

Oblinger, D. "Will E-business Shape the Future of Open and Distance Learning?" *Open Learning*, 2001, 16(1), 9–25.

Open Site. *The Dynamic Pricing Revolution*. [http://www.opensite.com/news/pdf/dprevolution.pdf]. 1999.

Peterson, R., Marostica, M., and Callahan, L. *E-Learning: Helping Investors Climb the e-Learning Curve*. Minneapolis, Minn.: U.S. Bancorp Piper Jaffray, 1999.

PricewaterhouseCoopers. *Technology Forecast: 1999*. Menlo Park, Calif.: PricewaterhouseCoopers Technology Centre, Oct. 1998.

Rappa, M. *Auctions*. [http://ecommerce.ncsu.edu:80/topics/auctions/auctions.html]. 2000a.

Rappa, M. *Business Models*. [http://ecommerce.ncsu.edu:80/topics/models/models.html]. 2000b.

Rappa, M. *Hypermarkets*. [http://ecommerce.ncsu.edu:80/topics/markets/markets.html]. 2000c.

Rappa, Michael. *Intelligent Agents*. [http://ecommerce.ncsu.edu:80/topics/agents/agents.html]. 2000d.

University Business. "Paperless Trail." *University Business*, July/Aug. 2000, *3*(6), 15–16.

Virtual University News. "Georgetown Auctions Seats in Multimedia Course." *Virtual University News*, Jan. 14, 2000, p. 4. 2000a

Virtual University News. "Ohio Launches Online Catalog." *Virtual University News*, Jan. 14, 2000, p. 4. 2000b

Virtual University News. "edu.com Raises $30 Million." *Virtual University News*, Feb. 2, 2000, p. 9. 2000c

Washington Post, Mar. 28, 2000.

7

Portal Technology Opportunities, Obstacles, and Options
A View from Boston College

Bernard W. Gleason

T he institutional information portal should be treated like a jewel in the crown. Every college and university has two very valuable assets: identity or brand name—such as Boston College—and loyal constituents—for example, alumni, students, parents, staff members, and prospective students. These assets need to be protected, and for this reason, Boston College concluded early on that the ownership and control of the institutional information portal would not be relinquished to an outside agency. One reason for reaching this conclusion is the desire to keep the portal free of commercialism. But a more important reason is that the institutional information portal is a key ingredient in the strategy and technical framework for transforming the university Web site into a customer-centric design.

There is great interest in institutional portals because the portal promises to be the user-elected point of entry that will provide all constituents with a single, personalized Web interface with all information and application resources in a secure, consistent, and customizable way. The portal also promises to be the means by which multiple devices and access methods can be used to provide access to new forms of information and new types of activities—providing convenient access to all appropriate information resources in an integrated manner anytime, anywhere.

Boston College has been an innovative leader in providing user access to personal information and to secure self-service transactions.

As we employ new advances in Internet and Web technologies, the focus is going to stay on self-service, but with an added dimension of full-service. The flexibility and scalability of the architecture of the institutional information portal is going to provide for the continuing evolution and inclusion of new capabilities—particularly e-business, e-learning, and the outsourcing of internal business process functions on an application-by-application basis. To meet these requirements the portal must ride on top of a middleware software infrastructure that will integrate and broker services to all applications for all users in a consistent manner (see Figure 7.1).

The institutional information portal is as important to the Web application architecture as the browser is to the client interface.

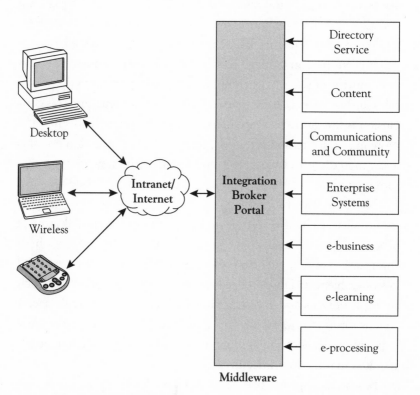

Figure 7.1. The Institutional Portal

The browser provides a common client and the portal provides a common framework—a framework that is based on an open architecture and is available to all applications to provide standard interfaces. The portal must be free and available to all constituents, just as the Web browser is free and available to the client on every desktop; there cannot be any fiscal impediments to customer participation. All constituents will have seamless access to all appropriate applications through a common portal framework without concern about the location or the operating environment of the application.

The emergence of the Internet and Web access to all university services will force institutions to rethink everything—from institutional image to systems architecture, new business and instructional models, and the information technology organization. As institutional leaders and technology experts, we need to step back, reflect, and think, and we need to take a university-wide perspective, with an eye toward the future. Moreover, we need to educate at all levels of the institutional management. The institutional information portal is going to be at the center of the transformation, but we cannot have a portal strategy unless we also have an institutional Web architecture and strategy—one with a "Big Picture" enterprise view.

In 1999, approximately twenty institutions possessed of a common vision of an open architecture to support customer-centric services, and recognizing the need both to protect their institution's image and to exploit the potential of the portal, joined together to form the Java in Administration Special Interest Group (JA-SIG). Since that time, institutional volunteers have been working actively and collaboratively to create a common portal reference framework called uPortal.

This chapter focuses on the strategic role of the common portal reference framework in the institutional Web architecture and will investigate the related management and institutional image issues.

What Is an Institutional Information Portal?

Institutional information portals in the commercial world are referred to as enterprise information portals and are derived from their more global counterparts (for example, Yahoo! and Netscape), which aggregate information from disparate sources. In an academic setting the corporate stigma is removed by substituting the word *institutional* for *enterprise*. Institutional information portals are applications that provide all members of the community with a single, intuitive, and personalized gateway to access and integrate campus-specific information, which is stored in the campus databases and systems, with externally stored information.

The campus Web site may be viewed as a collection of thousands of pages or department Web sites, but a portal is a collection of many applications, which are treated as separate channels. The portal provides a common entryway to many different applications with their own unique appearance and navigation. In the illustration in Figure 7.2, the boxes and labels are customized and personalized applications that will execute within the portal.

The mock-up in this figure is intended to provide a way to grasp the concept of all relevant information and services being delivered in a personalized and coherent form to an individual and to visualize possible functionality. It is only an illustration, and readers

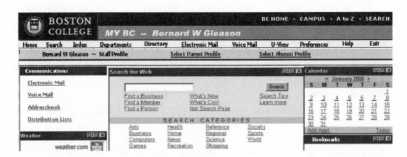

Figure 7.2. Institutional Information Portal Mock-Up

should not expend any time critiquing layout, colors, navigational structure, or content.

Initial implementations of campus portals were restricted to specific groups (such as students only) and to generally available information services (such as news and weather), communications (for example, e-mail), and online communities (for example, chat). Over the past few years colleges and universities have taken portals one step further and have begun to provide forms processing capabilities and secure access to enterprise systems (such as student and human resource records) and other personal information resources (such as calendars). Institutions are now faced with the challenge of providing expanded integrated capabilities, defining how the portal fits with the rest of the campus Web environment, and resolving the seemingly conflicting architectural designs of a customer-centric portal and the hierarchical structures of the traditional university Web site.

The portal requirements for secure services and integration are the same as the concepts for business-to-customer (B to C) e-business applications: single sign-on, cross-authentication and authorization across all applications, integration of all communications capabilities (such as e-mail) with applications, and seamless integration of all applications, regardless of whether the application is hosted on campus or off campus. In a campus environment, B to C could refer to business-to-constituent. As we move forward, our customers—all of our constituents—are going to expect that all information services will be accessible via the Web in a personalized and integrated form. We know generally where we need to be; it is now a matter of plotting the right course.

Institutional Web Strategy

The institutional information portal is at the center of the institutional Web strategy, and it represents a different way of organizing and structuring information based on the way in which individual constituents will want to interact with the university. The portal is not a silver bullet; it is a complementary component of the total institutional Web design, and it needs to be viewed as an integral element, not just as some add-on or as a competing technology. The portal represents a change in institutional philosophy in the delivery of services and a major shift to a customer-centric (portal-centric) design. In a portal-centric structure, the customer is the "star." Content and services are structured so that all constituents will use the portal as their prime entry point.

As shown in Figure 7.3, there are three main content views of the institutional Web architecture.

Public Web Site

At an institutional Web site, the top page, or institutional home page, is the primary entry page for external visitors and the general public. The top page sits at the top of the hierarchical organization of Web pages, and that view is presented in a structure defined by divisions, schools, departments, units, clubs, and so forth. Although each of these layers of the hierarchy may have a unique design, it is expected that the design and navigation of pages within a layer will be consistent. Traditionally, the coding and the management of content have been decentralized, with a loose linkage of all the components of the hierarchy. Because the pages are designed to service the general public, most information is not confidential and all content is available to everyone.

Colleges and universities are aware that the institutional Web site is now a major component of the institution's mass communication, marketing, recruiting, and fundraising efforts, and institutional image on the Web is an important consideration. It is now likely that the information on the Web is reaching a larger audience than are traditional print publications. At Boston College we have over one million visitors per month to the public Web site. The quality and accuracy of the presentation, as well as the organization of information on the public Web site, must now attain the same high standards as institutional print publications, and there is now

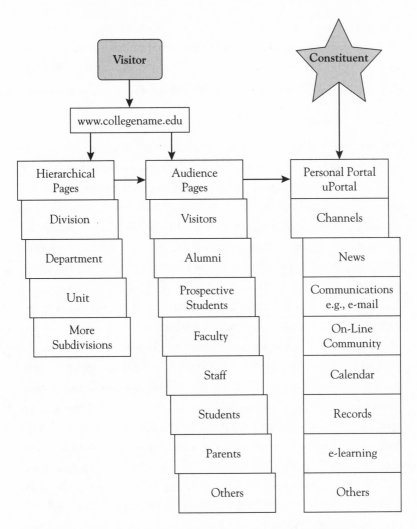

Figure 7.3. Three Main Content Views of Institutional Web Sites

a requirement to apply a consistent appearance and navigation structure across all of the top-layer pages of the institutional Web site.

The public institutional Web site contains two general categories of pages: institutional and personal. The institutional pages
are the pages that represent the official hierarchy and policies of the
university. For example, the home page of the chemistry department

and the admissions policies of the law school are institutional and should therefore conform to the institutional image, content design, and navigation strategy. But fraternity home pages and faculty personal Web pages do not need to conform.

Audience Pages

An institutional Web site is likely to contain thousands of individual Web pages, but only a segment of the total information content is pertinent to a particular visitor. For example, information regarding some internal operating procedures would not be of interest to a prospective student. From within the public Web site, constituents are able to self-elect a grouping (such as student, alumni, or faculty), and information content and navigation is customized for the designated audience. Visitors can link to any of the audience pages; they are not secure. For example, a prospective student may wish to experience the view of a matriculating student.

Each external audience or constituency usually has a specific, information-only audience page. For example, there are separate audience pages for parents, faculty members, and students. These audience pages all have a similar format and use the same consistent interface design and navigation scheme, and there is redundant general information as well as audience-specific content. The top page of the public Web site is designed for the external audience and casual visitors, and in this sense the top page of the institutional Web site is the "external" audience page. These audience pages will also contain instructions and a means for logging into a personal portal (institutional information portal) in order to access personalized, customized, and secure information and transaction processing capabilities.

Personal Portal

The personal portal takes the concept of audience pages a couple of steps further. The first and most important part of this architectural concept is that constituents log in to the portal to identify themselves. At Boston College all constituents (such as students, alumni, and parents) will authenticate against a central directory service called the lightweight directory access protocol (LDAP) with a combination of any standard Boston College identifier (eagle number, social security number, or user name) and personal identi-fication number (PIN). All constituents will be given credentials as soon as they are identified as an entity within the university.

Constituents will be easily enticed to log in because the portal log-in is standard; there will be nothing new to know or remember, with no new passwords or different passwords for every service. Indi-viduals may belong to multiple constituent groups (that is, the same person may be a staff member, a parent, and an alumnus), but he or she will only have one set of credentials—same ID and PIN and a single e-mail address. Providing credentials for everyone develops a greater sense of belonging to the BC community.

The directory service also contains profile information, access control privileges, and preference parameters for each person, so that the information content can be filtered for the specific indi-vidual in a secure and individualized manner. The only viewer of a personal portal page is the owner, so the issue of institutional image is irrelevant. The portal is customized to the individual, and func-tionality and convenience to the customer are the most important design considerations.

Access to secure services will not always be executed by logging into the personal portal. In instances when it makes sense to access a secure service from the public Web site or the audience structure, the application will continue to use the functionality of the portal infrastructure for directory services (authentication) and integra-tion. For example, Figure 7.4 shows a sequence of screen shots depicting how an alumnus entering the alumni association audience page could access secure on-line alumni community services that are hosted at a remote location.

This example demonstrates the application of the requirement to extend the institutional identity and image across the entire

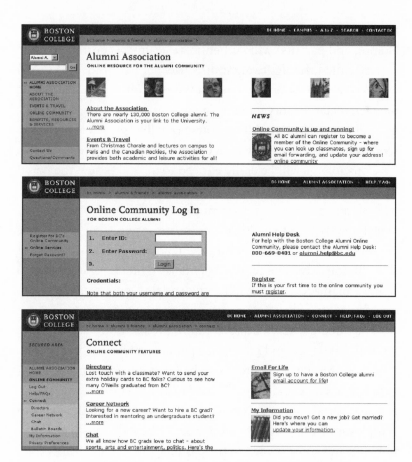

Figure 7.4. Example: Audience Page Links to Secure Service

design of the institution Web site, providing the customer with a high-quality appearance and a consistent navigation structure.

Newly integrated Web applications will cut across department lines and present information from multiple sources in a single presentation layer that is convenient for the customer. For example, a fully functioning student registration system would integrate data and present content from multiple sources and processes. The challenge for application developers will be to manage the content and services so that the components will mesh operationally and logically. The portal structure is an appropriate means of pulling these dispersed data sources together.

Audience and personal portal pages provide a needed virtual facility that is not always accommodated by the institutional hierarchy. For example, there is probably not an Office of Parents in the university hierarchy, but there is a need to organize and present information and services to parents in a meaningful and unified format in both audience pages and personal portal pages. Information on a personal portal page for individual parents may range from general campus news to proxy services to access their child's student account, to opportunities for making contributions to the university's capital campaign.

uPortal—Common Portal Reference Framework

At many colleges and universities there are multiple independent portal projects in process, and there is poor coordination, an absence of a standard technology architecture, and little managerial insight and control. This disjointed approach has resulted because there is no clear-cut definition of an institutional information portal and there is no technical guidance that will help software vendors and their customers build these information portals. At an early meeting of the JA-SIG, a discussion of portals and Web strategies was characterized by one of the institutional representatives as a "group therapy session." All the participating institutions were experiencing similar issues and consequently there were opportunities for common solutions.

The participating colleges and universities banded together to define a common portal reference framework—uPortal. The working group stipulated that the common portal reference platform must do the following:

- Provide access to all information and services through a single graphical interface

- Support a single log-on to obtain authentication and authorization to all information resources and applications

- Provide a framework in which all elements of the university (academic, administrative, and community) and all business applications can be integrated

- Provide a convenient set of communications services that are Web-based

- Provide a one-stop place where all members of the university community can perform all business transactions

- Provide the ability to present information and access to services on an individual basis in a personalized manner

- Provide each member of the community with the ability to customize the appearance, layout, and information on an individual basis

- Grant to the university full control and self-management of appearance and content

- Be vendor-independent (not locked into proprietary hardware or software)

- Be free of commercialization (no advertising or selling of products unless university-sponsored)

- Be available to all constituents twenty-four hours a day, seven days a week

- Be flexible and able to absorb new technology advances and new applications

The objective of uPortal is to provide a common framework and a set of channel standards to which application developers and commercial application vendors can write a standard, one-time-only interface. The first version of uPortal, which is available free of charge to all colleges and universities, was released in July 2000, and the beta version of uPortal 2.0 was released in late July 2001. The production version of this second release was scheduled to become available in November 2001. A number of other institutions are considering the adoption of uPortal as the institutional information portal framework and are undertaking appropriate evaluations of this tool. In October 2001, Campus Pipeline announced their adoption of uPortal as that company's portal framework.

What Are the Alternative Portal Strategies?

The topic of portals is "hot" on every campus, and information technology planners everywhere are busy sorting through the options and devising strategies for their institutions. For the sake of discussion, the options have been separated into the following groupings:

- Higher education portal vendor

- Enterprise resource planning (ERP) vendor

- Portal vendor with ERP affiliation

- Course Management System application vendor

- Portal software vendor

- In-house developed vendor (for example, Agora)

- Open source provider (for example, uPortal)

Over the past couple of years, colleges and universities were inundated with vendor proposals to provide their rendition of a campus portal at no charge to the institution. These portal vendors created hosted portal sites that were geared to the higher education market, and they derived their revenue from selling advertising banners or including prominent links to sites, which in turn sell products. These vendors marketed these so-called good deals to individual units within the campus in an attempt to get a foot in the door. The major marketing pitch of these vendors was that it would be too expensive for an individual institution to develop an enterprise portal on its own.

For smaller institutions, for some divisions within universities, or for some institutions that are only concerned about a limited population (for example, just students), the higher education portal option became an attractive short-term tactic. These institutions were able to become early adopters quickly with very little financial impact. At the same time, they surrendered control of the institutional image and constituent base. These institutions also tied themselves to a potentially unstable technology base and to a business model that may not be viable. For larger and more diversified institutions that are seeking an enterprise solution, affiliation with one of these vendors is not advised.

Enterprise resource planning vendors have entered the portal arena by offering products that integrate tightly with their ERP product offerings. These vendors, such as PeopleSoft and SCT, are building partnerships with a variety of content providers and profess to be building these products to be open. If an institution has the full range of application systems from a particular ERP vendor, it may also make sense to select the complementary portal product. This approach may of course lock an institution into a single proprietary vendor and establish dependency on a single vendor, whose interest may be more focused on growing market share than on serving the best interests of the university. An alternative and perhaps better long-term strategy is to employ a completely open portal that is part of the institution's middleware tier and separate from its back-end systems.

There is another group of vendors who are really the same as the ERP vendors. These vendors, most notably Jenzabar, started out as higher education portal vendors offering such community services as e-mail, chat, and news—and then they realized that they needed to address the customer demand for tighter linkage and access to institutional data systems. These vendors have in effect linked the portal with a suite of back-office software. With the acquisition of four back-end data system vendors—CARS, Quodata, CMDS, and Campus America—Jenzabar has chosen to solve the problem of gaining instant access to a customer base by attempting to meet the portal integration requirements of the users of these application systems. The institutions in this market segment are most often smaller colleges, which are more likely to relinquish some control of the portal framework for ease of implementation and management. For the same reasons previously cited for the ERP vendors, vendors in this category may not be an advisable selection for most large universities.

Many application vendors, particularly in the course management area, have been forced to create or license a portal framework to support their operating environment. Out of necessity, these application vendors, particularly Blackboard, have positioned their product set to be the campus portal solution. These course management vendors are on a similar strategy track as the portal designers; each is attempting to build and deploy an enterprise solution—the solution that will be used by everyone and will be completely Web-based. These application systems need an underlying portal component in their architecture, but the application system should not be the institutional portal unto itself. The application system should ride on top of an institutional information portal framework.

The pressure is on the application systems vendors to produce enterprise versions that integrate with the rest of the institution's information data sources and acquire basic authentication and authorization services from an institutional portal. Increasingly, vendors, out of necessity and from a vendor cost advantage, are supporting and adopting open systems efforts, such as uPortal. At the very least, these application vendors will need to provide compatibility between the application portal (for example, Blackboard) and the institutional information portal (for example, uPortal). In the future, the commitment by an application systems vendor to open integration will be a precondition for selection of enterprise application products.

A pure portal vendor, such as Plumtree, is another alternative for colleges and universities to consider. In fact, if institutions cannot wait for an acceptable production version of uPortal, or if the uPortal initiative is not successful, then the selection of one of these pure portal vendors would be going in a logical direction. One of the problems we faced in dealing with commercial software vendors was pricing structures and a lack of orientation to the higher education market. In the case of portal software that is going to be used by hundreds of thousands of constituents, when alumni and prospective students are considered, the per-user pricing models will never be acceptable.

JA-SIG launched the uPortal initiative because there was consensus among major university information technologists that there existed a need for a common portal reference framework—a framework that is based on open systems standards, is open-source, is free to all institutions, and is designed for higher education. By acting collectively and collaboratively, JA-SIG member schools are able to reduce costs and facilitate sharing, as well as consolidate the combined influence of most of the prestigious colleges and universities. For vendors, this initiative creates a strong inducement to provide a single, standards-based interface with the uPortal framework, thus eliminating further institutional integration costs. At the same time, institutions will be able to retain their individual identities and total control over their institutional Web sites.

Many universities are in a similar position in evaluating options. Should they wait on uPortal, develop an in-house institutional information portal, or adopt a commercial portal product? At Boston College our strategy is to continue to develop our internal portal, Agora (which has been in existence for about three years), to look to uPortal as the long-term solution, and to aggressively support the efforts of JA-SIG. If the uPortal initiative fails, then we will need to use an alternative method—either adopt a commercial portal product or continue to use Agora as an interim solution. In any case, our strategy is to own the portal and never consider turning the portal over to a third-party vendor.

Selling the Importance of the Portal Strategy

As designers and developers of the institutional information portal, we need the assurance that the enterprise approach is approved and accepted as an institutional strategy. We also need to alert and educate the institution as to the importance of the institutional information portal. But selling architecture is a lot harder than selling solutions. Business people want to see a working system, not a great conceptual design. Institutions are not adopting institutional information portals because they are impressed with underlying technology; in most cases they don't care about technology. Executives need a sound business strategy—one that is based on function and cost, not technology.

The most important question may be this: How do you get the highest levels of management focused on a set of interrelated strategies that are too complicated for most executives to understand but are critical to the central communications functions and operations of the university? Expecting executive management to grasp the technologies is unrealistic. Instead, we need to frame issues so that they appeal to the basic instincts of all good decision makers—such instincts as intuition, common sense, and the urge to be the best.

The traditional role of senior management of the university is to set and nurture long-term goals and strategies. The strategies include such areas as long-range fiscal planning, enrollment management, master planning for campus buildings, and athletic programs. In each of these examples the university has placed responsibility and trust in the hands of a knowledgeable individual or organizational unit. The same high-level, institutional focus should be applied to the Internet and the Web. In the unified adoption of Internet technologies and the Web, the role of a vice president, dean, or senior manager should be one of supportive endorser, not uninformed defender of individual or local interests.

Leadership and Institutional Issues

The institutional Web site is composed of integrated and interrelated pieces that are part of one giant system, and institutions need to recognize the impact and requirements of the central management of a distributed environment. The information technology leader needs to pursue the following objectives:

- Establish the institutional leadership for Web development and management

- Get the institutional Web and portal strategy defined, understood, and endorsed

- Establish the integrated Web architecture to support the top-down, enterprise model

- Clear up the roles of individuals within information technology and operating units on campus and establish a commitment to executing those roles

- Establish a central resource unit for the definition of standards and the ongoing management and monitoring of the institutional Web site

- Determine and orchestrate the rapid transition of the current Web environment to the institutional model for the future

- Eliminate the need for skilled, costly technicians to maintain Web content

Leadership in the development of the institutional Web strategy requires the full-time assignment of a single individual or a small, informed group of individuals. This leadership should provide a strategic, university-wide perspective on the role of the Web, in order to conceptualize the entire Web structure and information flow and to apply the proper technologies to meet the needs of the Web strategy. The current practices of disjointed planning and decision making can no longer be tolerated if an institution hopes to tap the real power and promise of the Internet and the Web to enhance the institutional image and to positively change the way in which the university functions.

The challenge of creating an institutional Web architecture can be summarized in two words: infrastructure and integration. When we line up the potential business projects that may be addressed using Internet and Web technology, we are likely to encounter the following questions:

- How do we develop a portal strategy if we don't have the required technology infrastructure in place?

- How will new Web applications be integrated with existing back-end legacy applications, such as PeopleSoft and in-house-developed enterprise systems?

- Will a new Web application use existing security services—such as authentication and authorization, or will we have to create a new set for every new application?

- How will new applications exchange data with new existing applications and existing databases? Will we have standard procedures or will we have proprietary interfaces for every new application?

- Where will each new application fit into the larger picture? Where is the application located on the institutional Web site and how does one get to it?

These questions and many more like them quickly lead knowledgeable technology architects to the obvious conclusion that there must be a common software infrastructure and that there must also be a common set of integration standards. Without a common framework and standards, there is chaos with very expensive and ineffective support costs.

Information technology staffs now need to focus effort and resources on the software infrastructure and the middleware layer to support systems and service integration, particularly the integration of Internet and Web services. There is also a need for corresponding change in the organizational structure and for the establishment of a separate unit composed of developers and innovators who possess in equal parts technical and soft skills (see Figure 7.5).

The responsibilities of the Internet services group are the following:

- Provide the vision and institutional leadership on campus for Internet and Web development and provide the single focal point for decision making

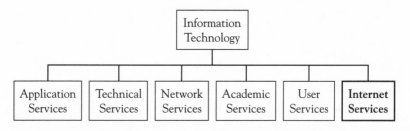

Figure 7.5. Information Technology Organization

- Develop the institutional Web strategy in conjunction with the university community and manage a top-down approach to design

- Build the institutional technical framework into which all Web applications will fit, and create and enforce the rules for integration of all applications

- Implement the software infrastructure and development tools to support an effective institutional Web site

- Provide leadership to the rest of the development community in the use and deployment of new technologies and directions (such as e-learning and e-business)

- Protect the institution's multimillion-dollar investment in existing systems and integration services (for example, single log-on, directory services, and role-based authorization)

- Ensure that the university is protecting the future and eliminating cost by adopting products and techniques based on nonproprietary standards

- Work with potential vendors to adapt products to meet the requirements of the university and open systems standards

- Work with other universities and vendors in consortium and partnership relationships to maximize resources and to leverage collective forces

Conclusion

This chapter attempts to share directions and personal opinions rather than list a set of issues and possible alternatives. Readers may not agree with many of the personal assessments and approaches, and many of the strategies and directions may not be a practical fit for another institution. However, sharing ideas is the key to building consensus within campus business and technical units, within the greater higher education community, and with business partners. Information technology leaders need to be prepared to express their views on critical issues such as the role of the institutional information portal in the institutional Web architecture. As we proceed with the inevitable discussions and decisions about the institutional portal strategy in the context of the institutional Web strategy, it is vital that information technology leaders be prepared to articulate the strategy in a comprehensive manner. People at all levels—from departmental managers to the president of the institution—will respect the depth of knowledge and vision.

It is important to cultivate this top-down, broad view rather than working from or reacting to individual bottom-up initiatives. In this respect, customers are principally interested in functionality and have little regard for the technical (hardware and software) infrastructure and the integration requirements. The result is that infrastructure and integration, to the dismay of informed and professional information technology staff, is being defined by default by the application solution. In most cases, because of this approach to product selection, information technology management is left to deal with the resulting internal human resource issues and very costly and unnecessary ongoing support requirements for these suboptimal systems.

Buy, Build, Integrate

Higher education's information technology professionals are really in the business of stitching things together, and the portal becomes the key integration component. Our customers, who do not either understand or care about the underlying architecture or back-end data structures that accomplish this integration, perceive integration through the so-called presentation layer. This is why the portal is indeed like a jewel in the crown. In this sense, uPortal can be thought of as a portal server; the desired components (channels) are served to the customer through the uPortal framework.

8

Portal Technology Opportunities, Obstacles, and Options

A View from the California State University

Steven L. Daigle and Patricia M. Cuocco

What is a portal? A portal is a gate, a door, or entrance. In the context of the World Wide Web, it is the next logical step in the evolution toward a digital culture.

Portals have become one of the most visible information technology (IT) issues in higher education, as well as the commercial sector. The latest Gartner International *hype cycle* curve places portals at its apex. That firm estimates that at least 5 percent of U.S. higher education institutions will have partially or fully implemented portals by Fall 2000. By 2006, Gartner predicts that 80 percent of universities with a thousand or more students will have enterprise portals. According to Merrill Lynch, the total corporate portal market reached $4.5 billion last year and is projected to reach $14.8 billion by 2002.

This chapter provides an executive university readership with an understanding of portals and offers an overview of portal benefits, together with the potential problems and policy issues associated with them. It does not explain portal technology but describes some basic design principles, and it is offered as a starting point for developing a coherent, campus-wide portal strategy. Some options are offered as to how campuses might proceed, either individually or as part of a university system.

As defined by IBM, an Internet portal is "a single integrated, ubiquitous, and useful [point of] access to information (data), applications, and people" (IBM, 2000). A portal may look like a Web site, but it is much more than that. Although a Web site is an important part of any university's communications strategy, it is primarily a way to provide static information.

Christopher Connolly of Villanova University writes that "a portal . . . is a gateway to the Web that allows the plethora of information available on Internet and Intranet Web sites to be organized and customized through a single entry point. A good portal provides seamless access for non-authenticated users until sensitive information is requested, when it then prompts for a username and password. Authenticated visitors or those known to the site by cookies (textual information passed to the client to be stored on the client's system) are presented with a more individualized view of the organization's Web site" (2000, p. 38). A portal "knows" the individual using it, and it changes with the individual; it is an individual's personal assistant or proactive agent, ready to act on his or her behalf.

As Strauss suggests, there are three kinds of portals:

1. *Vertical portals*, which provide access to a variety of information and services about a particular area of interest. For example, Wine.com is a vertical portal. Such portals offer information and services customized for niche audiences (such as undergraduates, faculty members, and alumni).

2. *Horizontal portals*, which are often referred to as "megaportals." These portals target the entire Internet community. Sites such as Yahoo.com, Lycos.com, and Netscape.com are megaportals. These sites always contain search engines and provide the ability for a user to personalize the page by offering various channels (for example, access to other information, such as regional weather, stock quotes, or news updates). Providers of megaportals hope individual users will go to their sites first, to access the rest of the Internet. Their financial models are built on a combination of advertising and "click-through" revenues.

3. *University or enterprise portals*, which can be either *vertical*—
   focusing on a specific application, such as human resources,
   accounting, or financial aid information, or *horizontal*—offering
   access to almost all the information an individual within the
   university needs to carry out his or her function. Authentication and access are based upon the role or roles the individual
   plays in the organization. Horizontal enterprise portals (HEPs)
   can be customized and personalized. If properly designed, they
   can replace much of the user's computer desktop.

Like a TV remote control, portals offer a number of channels.
These might include reports and documents needed for class assignments, calendars, such administrative information as grades and
degree audits, campus news and events, collaboration and discussion groups, reference material and links to other sources, and personal leisure, financial, or family information. Portals represent the
next logical step in home page, Intranet, and general Web evolution because they integrate all three.

In addition to a sophisticated search engine, portal development
and implementation depend on a number of interrelated technologies: authentication and security, caching, automated taxonomy
engines, application integration middleware, relational databases,
and metadata dictionaries. Many of these are "under the hood"
technology functions but are essential for enabling e-services and
for evaluating vendor alternatives. This chapter focuses on HEPs in
a university environment.

Should a University Have a Portal?

A Web portal may be the answer to a question that has not been
and may never be asked. However, the hype surrounding portals, as
well as the plethora of vendors knocking on the door, makes them
impossible to ignore. Compelling reasons to develop a portal are
that an increasingly Internet-savvy student body expects it, and the

horse is already out of the barn. It would be hard to find a campus where someone—whether in the alumni association, in sports, in university development, or in a large academic department—has not either built his or her own portal or ordered one. This may have occurred without the knowledge, coordination, and assistance of the institution's chief information officer or another in campus executive management.

In the heyday of enthusiasm about the so-called New Economy, portal vendors often approached higher education executives with promises of revenue generation, cradle-to-grave (or at least application-to-endowment) relationships with students, and productivity gains for all university constituencies. Although financial benefits may be a potential outcome, revenue generation also involves broader policy questions about the appropriateness of advertising on an academic portal. Still other e-commerce applications may generate privacy concerns. Individual campuses engaged in selling merchandise or services on the Web may also run the risk of complaints from local businesspeople, who may object to competition from a public institution. For these reasons, it is doubtful if revenue generation should be the primary reason for development of a university portal.

However, all universities are likely to someday use portal technology. The key questions are *when* and *how*. Developing a campus portal is a strategic technology decision that will affect the entire campus community. The decision on a portal strategy requires careful analysis of long- and short-term needs.

Who Will Benefit from a Portal, and How Will They Benefit?

Whether the campus is looking for recognition, ease of operations, productivity gains, cost savings, or a combination of these, the portal will succeed or fail based upon the perceived benefits to the university community. The portal should make it easier and more efficient for every stakeholder to carry out his or her role in the institution.

One obvious reason for deploying portals is to improve productivity by increasing the speed and customizing the content of information provided to internal and external constituencies. Portals also serve a knowledge management function by dealing with information glut in an organized fashion. In some ways, portals offer a technical solution, but not a total answer, to knowledge management. Creating the potential for campus constituents to personalize and tailor their preferred sources of information is a powerful step in the right direction.

Another real benefit is that many of the technical issues that must be addressed in a portal implementation (such as authentication, authorization, security, and messaging) are aligned with efforts to build out the technology infrastructure. Those issues (often referred to as middleware) are central to a robust inter- and intra-campus network and end-to-end Internet connectivity.

University portals can be a means for individuals to establish a long-term relationship with the institution. In particular, portals provide views of the institution that reflect an individual's relationship at various stages of his or her life. A patient of the university's hospital sees less of that university than do students, staff members, parents, and others. Portals facilitate the presentation of the institution's many faces. They not only make it easy to do business, they also allow for interaction and collaboration among students, faculty members, staff members, and alumni with similar needs and interests. Properly implemented, portals can be strategic assets for institutions. In that sense, they do far more than traditional Web sites of static information ever could.

Beyond institutional gains, portals offer obvious benefits to students, faculty members, staff members, and external stakeholders.

Students benefit from

- Web interface with courseware and required information about courses

- Increased and easier communications with faculty members

- On-line access to grades, financial aid information, class schedules, and graduation checks

- Access to the communities of interest within the university, such as sports, clubs, and community service opportunities

- Increased lifelong learning opportunities

Faculty and staff members benefit from

- Real-time communications with students

- Simplified course management tools

- Instant access to information for advising students

- Easily accessible information for every facet of their job

How Does an Institution Get Started?

At this point, the challenge is not to get started, but, rather, to corral the disparate efforts on campus and take a unified approach to portals. This may involve some level of executive intervention.

A consensus seems to be emerging among students of portal development concerning best practices and potential obstacles. The major points of agreement include the following:

- There should be one and only one horizontal portal on campus. Theoretically, each member of the university community will sign on to the portal every day, whether to access class schedules, class notes, homework assignments, calendars, e-mail, or daily task lists. This point does not preclude the possibility, indeed the probability, of several vertical portals being nested behind the single horizontal enterprise portal.

- It should be built iteratively. First-generation portals emphasize content; second-generation portals focus on institutional processes, services, technology applications, and process integration; third-generation portals will likely strive to integrate data, voice, and video on a variety of platforms (such as handheld computers), perhaps over wireless networks.

- There should be a single sign-on for each individual, regardless of his or her campus role. That sign-on should be designed so that an individual can access whatever information he or she is permitted to have, including access to the vertical portals. The sign-on should follow the user through any campus vertical portals.

- The sign-on should allow for the possibility of overlapping roles. For example, some students are part-time employees, some staff members are either part-time students or alumni, administrators may be part-time faculty members, and so forth.

- Institutions should consider both academic and administrative legacy systems, as well as newer applications. Campuses should neither build nor buy a portal without having a clearly defined strategy for migration from legacy systems to new software, either with the design team or with the vendor. This strategy should be communicated to the campus community.

- Because the goal of a portal is to be a single, seamless interface with all necessary applications, whatever course software packages a campus uses should interface with the portal. To the extent possible, campuses should attempt to limit the number of course software packages that will be supported by the portal.

- Although revenue generation should not be the driving force behind development of a portal, the design should not preclude revenue from advertising or e-commerce applications.

Who Are the Leading Vendors and What Do Portals Cost?

The portal vendor industry is in the early stages of development. Major shakeouts occur on a near-monthly basis among the roughly one hundred vendors. The risk for any institution in choosing a vendor under these conditions is considerable.

Gartner International estimates that it could cost an institution anywhere from $50,000 to $250,000 for a portal license fee, plus 15 to 20 percent for maintenance. Services and training can cost two to four times the price of the license fee. Accordingly, they recommend that institutions always deploy and test a pilot system first, and then build the basic functions of content integration, database and applications integration, and process integration in an iterative fashion. Other critical functions—such as security, caching, taxonomy development, searching, and personalization—should also be approached in phases rather than all at once. Gartner goes on to suggest that although there are plenty of visionary and niche players in the portals market arena, there still are no leaders in the industry and no challengers.

Portal Provider Options
for Higher Education in 2001?

Typically, a portal should provide personalized access to information, integrated access to data systems and attendant applications, and process integration between individual schedules and institutional calendars (often the most difficult requirement to satisfy).

Selecting a portal source has become very complex and risky. It is interesting to note that one informal survey of fifty U.S. research universities showed a *reduced* penetration of this technology between May 2000 and May 2001.[1] From July 2000 to July 2001, a number of commercial suppliers entered and exited the commercial marketplace. Early enthusiasm for financing the portal investment through the recovery of advertising and click-through charges has in general yielded to a more narrow and conservative definition of portal products and to cost recovery through traditional licensing fees or through bundling of portal products with other products, such as enterprise resource planning (ERP) systems. Increasingly, the commercial choice among vended portal products requires due diligence regarding the business viability of the portal suppliers under consideration.

Another major factor in choosing a portal vendor is the extent of a supplier's business partnerships and relationships, both horizontal and vertical. A successful portal vendor must borrow from the best practices of companies that specialize in critical areas, such as content providers, systems integrators, search engines, operating systems, middleware, and even mobile networks.

Table 8.1 lists eight portal vendors in this volatile market that were active in higher education between July 2000 and July 2001, together with brief descriptions of their revenue models and key selling points. Obviously, the advertising and e-commerce features of these products are both controversial and uncertain and could involve higher education institutions in matters beyond their

Table 8.1. Some Portal Vendors in Higher Education

Providers	Revenue Model	Differentiators
Blackboard	Bundled with Level 3; e-commerce optional	Productivity tools, revenue sharing; Datatel alliance
Campus Cruiser	Ads, e-commerce, fees	Productivity tools, revenue sharing; Datatel alliance
Campus Pipeline	Ads, e-commerce, fees, sponsorship	Integration APIs, local hosting, SCT & WebCT alliances
Jenzabar	E-commerce, fees, sponsorship	Own four higher education ERP companies, instructional support, nonenterprise accounts
Mascot Network	Limited ads, e-commerce, fees, connectivity revenue	Community niche orientation, free implementation, coexistence strategy
PeopleSoft Portal	Free to PS customers; e-commerce optional; fees	Preintegration with PS; community tools alliance with iSun
uPortal	Community sourced	JA-SIG sponsorship; JAVA-based architecture; IBS partnership
Z University	Ads, sponsorship, e-commerce	Focus on alumni relations niche; revenue sharing

By the time of publication, some of these commercial portal providers had exited the market.

expertise or interest. However, in the words of Looney and Lyman, "the entrepreneurial world has looked around the Internet and realized that the most connected population with the best commercial demographics is in higher education" (2000, p. 33). The e-commerce implications of portals will never be far away, however much some may wish them to be. The challenge for higher education is to adapt portal technology intended for commercial purposes to academic pursuits and academic virtual communities.

In addition to commercial vendors, the Java in Administration Special Interest Group (JA-SIG) has released the first portal framework designed by and for higher education institutions. Created in part through funding from the Andrew Mellon Foundation, uPortal combines a set of technical specifications and software designed to allow institutions to build customized portals using a publish-and-subscribe interface and functional channels developed and shared among the uPortal user community. The software is available for download, free of charge from the JA-SIG clearinghouse site at JA-SIG.org. At this writing, the production version of this product was released in late 2001.

The potential advantages of uPortal are lower costs, compared with commercial products, and greater institutional control over content. uPortal requires a Java-capable programming staff that is available to support the framework's implementation. Community sourcing is the key feature of and the key challenge to JA-SIG. Although community sourcing spares much of the cost of in-house development, uPortal still requires significant interface design, and users may have to develop their own channels. As of this writing, nine universities were operating either production or test uPortal sites.

Although there will be frequent leapfrogging in this new area of technology development, based on discussions in the professional literature, the following universities are among those with the most well-developed portals in higher education. Together, they offer a variety of design formats, content, and funding alternatives. Their experiences should inform any campus decision.

- University of Washington—MYUW—http://myuw.washington.edu

- UCLA—MYUCLA—http://www.my.ucla.edu

- Boston College—uPortal—http://www.ja-sig.org

- LSU—PAWS—http://paws.lsu.edu

- University of Minnesota—My ONE STOP—http://onestop.umn.edu

- University of British Columbia—MYUBC—http://my.ubc.ca

- University at Buffalo—MyUB—
  http://www.buffalo.edu/aboutmyub

In the final analysis, portal deployment is much like anything else—one can have it fast, have it good, or have it cheap. The catch is that only two out of three are possible.

What Policy Issues Should Be Considered?

In the current environment, extreme due diligence is the only protection against the volatility of the portal industry. If an institution can wait to deploy a portal, it should wait until a likely consolidation among vendors and price competition occurs. Moreover, the portal industry has not yet reached agreement on certain basic standards. If a university cannot wait, then the following questions and issues should be considered:

- *What short-term problem is the campus attempting to solve with a portal? Why is the portal the only, or the best, solution?*

- *Is executive management willing to mandate a single portal for the campus?* A portal can be a tool for building a virtual campus community. It can also drive process transformations that result in cost efficiencies. Multiple nonintegrated portals defeat both of these purposes.

- *Does executive management understand, and is it willing to communicate to the campus, that the investment in a portal is not a one-time event?* Portals require a continuous investment as they evolve and migrate from interfacing with legacy systems to interfacing with new software systems and all of the version changes inherent therein.

- *Who "owns" what data and how will conflicts between data owners be resolved? Who manages the portal?* The CIO is (or should be) the person on campus charged with the resolution of conflicts among data "owners." The CIO ultimately should be responsible for access to all information systems and the seamless integration of these systems for presentation through the HEP.

- *Is advertising appropriate on an academic HEP?* Each campus must make this determination for itself. The answer will be driven by a number of factors, not the least of which is campus culture.

- *Is e-commerce acceptable through the campus HEP?* E-commerce is a far broader topic than can be addressed here. There are aspects of e-commerce that are already commonplace on campuses. These include on-line catalogs and on-line purchasing, electronic funds transfer, and bill payments.

One example of e-commerce is an arrangement between the campus and Amazon.com, where every time an individual accesses the on-line bookseller through the campus portal, the campus receives a small percentage of the purchase price of goods. This could pose a potential conflict with the campus bookstore and other campus auxiliaries. Another issue that should be considered relative to e-commerce is competitive pressure from local businesspeople.

Other policy considerations include

- *Security and ensuring the privacy of student and employee data.* These have always been serious issues. However, when the possibility exists for a single sign-on to virtually every existing university information system, security becomes more than a line in someone's job

description. It becomes mission critical and the responsibility of every campus employee.

- *Intellectual property.* This could become as big an issue
  in portal deployment as infrastructure integration (for
  example, witness the Napster controversy). This is an
  especially sensitive issue for faculty members, and
  policies should be established in advance of
  deployment.

Want a Portal? What's Next?

There are at least three routes to portal development. The first is to
build it. Experts are nearly unanimous in arguing against this
approach because development and maintenance of a "homegrown" product can be a problem. The second option is to purchase
a preintegrated, packaged product. The third alternative is to purchase a portal service—in effect, to outsource. The choice among
these alternatives is complex and is rooted in the culture, traditions,
infrastructure, and workforce of the institution.

Each approach has opportunities and challenges. Developing
institution-specific solutions will likely result in a highly tailored solution but will often cause the campus to lag the marketplace as new
functions and features emerge in the commercial marketplace. Commercial portal functionality is driven by a larger marketplace, and the
pace of innovation in portal technologies is often driven by sectors
other than higher education. The integration of custom-developed
portal technologies may enhance interoperation with other campus-
developed software applications, or it may necessitate painful adap-
tations to vended applications in use by the institution.

Buying is also not a risk-free proposition. Vendors have various
financial models. Some depend on advertising revenue, whereas
others depend on click-through revenues for e-commerce. Still others offer a model by which the institution is charged for the num-

ber of Web pages the constituents access. All of these vendors will sell their products outright—usually at a very high price. These are not turnkey systems, and they still require technical support and expertise on the part of campus personnel.

Another potential pitfall is the relative immaturity of the industry. These are dot-coms in the truest sense, fraught with all the problems recently reported in the news. Most have seen the wisdom of partnering with larger, more experienced firms. However, in some cases the partnership dictates the "back room" system or course software solution, severely limiting campus choice. Everyone claims that their product can interoperate with everything else. As with all other enterprise software decisions, *caveat emptor*.

Note

1. Survey of participants in EDUCAUSE and NACUBO forums, May 2000 and May 2001. In May 2000, 25 percent of invited participants indicated that their institution had implemented an "enterprise information portal." In May 2001, 20 percent answered the same question affirmatively. The sample sets in this survey did not match completely, but the results and ensuing discussion suggest an atmosphere of cautious enthusiasm among participating information and business officers.

References

Connolly, C. "From Static Website to Portal." *EDUCAUSE Quarterly*, 2000, 23(2), 38–43.

IBM Global Education Industry. "Higher Education Portals: Presenting Your Institution to the World," Sept. 2000.

Looney, M., and Lyman, P. "Portals in Higher Education." *EDUCAUSE Review*, 2000, 35(4), 28–37.

Phifer, G. "Portal Products 2000 Magic Quadrant," Gartner Group Research Note, Sept. 29, 2000.

9

The Organizational Challenge

IT and Revolution in Higher Education

John R. Curry

Will we get it right the next time around? Will we actually migrate our revolutionary rhetoric toward useful and welcome new business processes that truly transform? Or will we temper our rhetoric? How can we business and technology leaders and managers systematically and continuously achieve better, measurable, and sustainable new administrative practices in colleges and universities? Or, what are we learning from our mistakes—and successes?

Lessons of the Nineties

Let's look at the recent track record of business process and information technology change initiatives. For me, "recency" begins with Hammer and Champy's *Reengineering the Corporation* (1993), or perhaps earlier, with Hammer's article "Reengineering Work: Don't Automate, Obliterate" (1990). The early nineties, infused with the fear of very real and extraordinary industrial competition from Japan, gave rise to volumes of papers and books in the management literature that make the case for rapid and disruptive change and offer new tools and techniques for organizational transformation. Business process mapping and design, workflow, technology-enhanced business transactions, e-commerce, the revival of "information is power" as "instant information is not fast enough," self-directed teams, empowered employees (no, knowledge workers!)—all these ideas, new, old, or transmogrified, informed the new management order, and created a whole new genre of consulting capabilities and organizations.

Higher education in the early nineties was fertile ground for sowing these new seeds of change management. The national economy was in the tank, states were drastically reducing budget allocations to their namesake universities, federal research support was flagging, revised rules governing recovery of benefit and administrative "indirect" costs shifted research costs to other sources of revenue, financial aid budgets were falling short of meeting need as the economy sapped families' ability to pay high private college and university tuition, and enrollments declined at many institutions across the country. The slogan "It's the economy, stupid!" defined the winning campaign strategy for the 1992 presidential election. Colleges and universities were in big budget trouble.

Their presidents and chief financial and information officers came to believe that if American industry could transform itself into a more efficient and competitive mode, then so could—indeed, so should—colleges and universities, to achieve efficiencies consistent with a diminished and limited resource base. And they looked for guidance to the new management literature, written for and about for-profit businesses. In some institutions, becoming lean, modern, and mean, when seen in the context of a national competitiveness crisis, rose to the level of moral imperative.

Thus did concepts and buzzwords such as business process reengineering, technology-leveraged paperless transactions, e-commerce, consolidated purchasing partnerships, and technology-literate knowledge workers come to embody the guiding concepts for reducing budgets and improving efficiency and service. Teams were formed. Documents were produced. In my world of the University of California at the time, these included Young's *Transforming Administration at UCLA* (1991), *Sustaining Excellence in the 21st Century* (1991), and *Developing a 21st-Century Workforce for California Government*

(1998). But kindred blueprints for radical change sprung up across the country without regard for state boundaries.

And then a third cosmic event aligned itself with the earlier two to create the perfect storm: Y2K. Lurking among thousands of lines of code, perhaps orders of magnitude more, in poorly documented, mostly homegrown software, were two-digit date placeholders that could not discern what century we were in when 99 turned to 00. Enterprise business applications had to be rewritten or replaced, and in a big hurry!

The logic of events was now this: we cannot ask governments for more money in a weak economy when our comrades in business have so boldly tackled their own transformation. We therefore have to reduce costs to live within our means and do so rationally; the cuts needed are too large to achieve across the board. Management scholars and consultants have shown us the tools, and businesses have shown the way. Because we have to rewrite or replace major enterprise business application software against an implacable deadline, we should further hew to the business model by installing off-the-shelf, industrial-standard systems (for example, SAP, Oracle, PeopleSoft, and Banner) and reengineer our processes around them (or vice versa)—all before December 31, 1999.

We assembled our business plans, showing large capital investments for hardware, software, network upgrades, and consultants, all repaid in relatively short order by sustained savings in administrative and purchasing costs. The benefits would live beyond the project's amortization period, providing improved services all the while. Governing boards blessed the plans. We formed project teams and donned project logo caps and tee shirts. We were off to the revolution. In the immortal words of one consultant, "the train is leaving, stragglers will be shot!"

The victory parades have been long in coming. Somewhere along the tortured paths to new processes and technologies, we met the enemy. And it was us: the management, faculty, and staff of our colleges and universities. Within every business process lurked personal territories, local traditions, someone's meaning of life, and bragging rights. For every new professional expectation envisioned by central administrators, there seemed to be a dissonant departmental service expectation defined by faculty members. With each newly touted capability of an enterprise system came defenses of locally grown shadow systems for their unique service to a unique clientele. Each new opportunity for shared information across organizational units or segments of a business process spawned concerns of confidentiality, or territorial disputes about data ownership and control. Consolidation of vendors to achieve better prices threatened friendships and unique service relationships. The "e" in e-commerce was easier promised than delivered because of incompatibilities across information technologies among vendors and universities.

Then, too, we underestimated how much complexity twenty years of accretion can burden a business process with, and we overestimated how suitable the off-the-shelf enterprise applications were to our innately complex institutions. We had to learn at very high hourly rates how little consultants understood us. All this conspired to bloat project budgets, wreck implementation schedules, and challenge our credibility! We often learned, too late, that senior leaders were not necessarily comrades in arms in the revolution. They were together when talk was cheap and apart when the going got tough and blame was in the air. We were in territory that the new tools were not designed to handle.

What We Are Learning Now

We were in *our* territory, however, and beginning to understand that the tools necessary for managing change might just lie somewhere in sociology, social psychology, cultural anthropology, economics, and organization theory. We were learning what Kurt Lewin (1999) said long ago: that you cannot understand an organization until you try to change it. We were learning an old lesson: it's the people, stupid!

I do not want to appear cynical here, especially since I have been in the midst of leaders, and often myself in leadership roles, in this attempted revolution—and proud of it! My goal in this chapter is the elucidation of a few maxims or tactics to guide our change initiatives in the future. To arrive at this point, we need only add a brief assessment of specific achievements and failures in our recent quest for revolutionary results.

Many colleges and universities have succeeded in their software implementations. By and large, this was a technological rather than organizational triumph, more a testimony to the skill and tenacity of programmers and information technology staff members than to the change management prowess of us leaders and managers. Many new business process designs still lie gathering dust in war room closets. The new software often re-reified old processes, or it gave shadow systems a new lease on life, or both. Some would say that the new systems paved the cow paths. Organizational obstacles to effecting new ways—decentralized authority, academic governance, unaligned leaders, fear and loathing—overwhelmed logic and institutional will. On the other hand, many obsolete systems are gone, and the new systems provide contemporary platforms for further development. That's a real accomplishment. But many of our original business goals remain elusive and our political capital has eroded.

We also convinced most major enterprise software application vendors to recognize, at least in part, unique research university requirements, such as grants management, labor distribution, and multiple sources of pay in their newer releases. Thus they are coming to recognize us as a key customer sector. That's a real accomplishment.

Many of us solved the information access problem—vendors really oversold their products' so-called report writers—by designing and investing in data warehouses. Although costly, warehouses enabled us to make good on the original reengineering promise of information access on user terms. We are now filling the warehouses with data from older systems, thus glimpsing the potential for integrated data generated from our (still) many and unintegrated software applications. And user acceptance has reduced the number of reasons not to continue moving forward with other modules of our chosen enterprise applications by at least one: the rage over unrequited expectations for instant and easily accessible data. That's a real accomplishment.

E-commerce marches forward on our campuses, inexorably if incrementally, even as the recent dot-com implosion has let some air out of the portal hot air balloon, thereby vastly reducing numbers of potential vendor-catalog aggregators and thwarting our eternal quest for comprehensive comparison shopping. This is yet another accomplishment, still well short of our aspirations and dissonant with our original rhetoric.

Those of us who replaced aging legacy systems with off-the-shelf enterprise software, never wanting to experience such upheaval again, have convinced ourselves (and our institutions) to obviate obsolescence by systematically installing vendor upgrades. Thus we are using external pressures from our vendors and our peer vendor user groups to do the right internal things—a powerful tool for sustaining technological currency. Which is quite an accomplishment. Moreover, software upgrades, when pursued relentlessly, teach our organizations that change—especially in technology—is continuous rather than episodic. This is a lesson in the virtue of relentless incrementalism as a management maxim, about which more later.

Our recent accomplishments—indeed our daring to take on revolutionary goals—are very much a consequence of the times and of timing, with hard times being aggravated by an external competitive threat, as well as by the rarest of timing—the first millennial threat to the functioning of our enterprise software. I doubt that we would have attempted or accomplished as much in the absence of such a unique hostile environment. So we should never forget the utility of these words from William Shakespeare, arguably one of the greatest organization theorists: "There is a tide in the affairs of men, which taken at the flood leads on to fortune."

If we attribute our success to surfing the tides of the nineties and the expiration of a century, how do we account for our failures? Why did so many of our business process and organizational change efforts founder? Why did we not save the annual millions attaching to all those superfluous steps we eliminated between old and new business processes? A simple answer is this: we took too many of our cues from the abstractions of the business process and information technology and not enough from theories of organizational behavior. We thought of revolution and technology rather than incremental change and human behavior.

That people and subunits in organizations are not innate utility maximizers was argued cogently over thirty-five years ago by Herbert Simon (1965). Indeed, Simon introduced "administrative man," who "satisfices" rather than maximizes, and whose rationality is "bounded" rather than comprehensive. Such notions were further explored and extended by Richard Cyert and James March, with the publication of A Behavioral Theory of the Firm (1963). Challenging the traditional economic theory of the firm, they studied and characterized actual decision processes. Incomplete information, conflicting organizational and subunit goals, conflict resolution through breaking down complex interrelated problems into smaller manageable unrelated ones, incremental decision making and organizational learning characterized by many traversals of the action-feedback-reaction loop, the importance of limited time and attention in the face of too many demands—these notions replace the economic model of subunits locally maximizing, which is consistent with the utility function of the firm.

Approximately a decade later, Michael Cohen and James March extended the lineage of behavioral theory into the realm of quintessential complexity, the modern university, in Leadership and Ambiguity: The American College President (1974). Universities did not just exhibit inconsistent goals and internal conflict, they were "organized anarchies"—organizations that in a fundamental operational sense did not know what they were doing. Attempting to characterize decision making—getting things done—in such a world, Cohen and March developed the "garbage can model," according to which, decisions emerge from the intermittent participation of people among changing issues (garbage in the can) over time, all in the context of nonoperational goals and scarcity of time, and hence individual attention. Among other things, they deduce from this model that sailing is the better leadership metaphor than power boating; that is, successful leadership lies in using the winds and currents to reach one's destination rather than racing through them in a straight line. Does this sound familiar? Thus we discover why working as administrators in universities leaves us perplexed and delighted.

Karl Weick (1979) uses the phrase "loosely coupled worlds" to describe organizations like ours: loose confederations of academic departments loosely coupled with each other and with central administrative units. In such worlds, people learn and change through imitation of others and through testing or playing with new ideas at the margins to see what works and what is fun. To reduce the complexity inhering in their environment, people impose their worldviews on data, thus seeing what they believe. In his studies of organizational cultures, Edgar Schein (1999) observes a variation on this theme: people will not recognize you as a professional until they trust you as a person. They will not *see* what you have to offer until they *believe* in you. Schein further observes that change efforts fail if the individuals' (and subunits') survival and learning anxieties are raised too high, and that learning anxiety must be reduced by increasing individuals' sense of "psychological safety."

Lessons for Change Management

So much for simplistic synthesis of a rich and complex literature. Let me take the perilous next step of distilling all this into three easy lessons:

1. People learn and change incrementally, and so do organizations. Internalize this.

2. Universities are deeply decentralized, loosely coupled by nature. Don't fight it; get used to it. Don't lament departmental balkanization; find ways to use it.

3. Knowing people and their organizational cultures is a necessary condition for transformative change. Never forget.

And what change management maxims or tactics can we deduce from these lessons?

- *Embrace relentless incrementalism as the change approach of choice.* Like compounding interest, organizational change will happen faster than you imagine, since incrementalism is a natural act. Measured increments also create structured opportunities to learn as you go and constantly refine strategies and realign leaders as you learn what works and where you are really headed. Incrementalism is tacking, the action-feedback-reaction loop is institutionalized. Revolutionary rhetoric, on the other hand, feeds survival anxiety and thus resistance to change. Suppress it.

- *Walk a mile in the shoes of those whose roles you would change.* Understand their worlds and learn what they need from you. Iterate between your expectations and their needs. Walk in many different shoes, and often. Teach each other. Become comrades.

- *Continuously build trust.* This is the most important and time-consuming responsibility we have. You can't make sustainable change without it. Communication, including the building of personal relationships, is the watchword.

- *Create "demand pull" for change rather than "supply push."* This will be counterintuitive to the technology wonks in our IT centers.

- *Lead change from the business rather than the technology side of the house.* It is the way we do our business that needs changing. Make the business case compelling so that others will embrace the goals. Technology may be the means, but it is not the end. Think people first, process second, organization third, and technology fourth.

- *Create local change champions and make them part of project leadership.* All good people want to do better and know many of the changes that will improve their work lives. If you partner with them, you can jointly champion an agenda. And local administrators will listen to (and trust!) their peers more than they will you. After all, they have walked more than a mile in the same shoes! But don't let the local champions forget their organizational roots. They need to keep the common touch as they "walk with kings" on behalf of the whole.

- *Use timing and the times to advance the pace of change.* Sometimes getting on bandwagons is the right thing to do. Choose bandwagons carefully. Look for moments of organizational instability—changes in leadership or budget crises, for example—to advance your change agenda as a preferred solution.

- *Create role models and pilot implementations; facilitate peer pressure for change.* Sometimes change is too overwhelming to contemplate in the abstract. Seeing others follow new ways and use new tools can reduce anxiety and motivate emulation. Design or join peer groups. As noted earlier, for example, membership in vendor-specific user groups creates peer pressure to implement software upgrades (new release), thus forcing relentless incremental improvements in user functionality and sustaining technological currency. A related tactic is:

- *Be an exemplar: Do to yourself first what you would do to others*. Doing is more impressive than saying. You will create believers if you can exhibit, within your own span of authority, the virtues of the new ways you espouse.

- *Align central and local incentives for change*. If the economies of change do not naturally redound to the benefit of those local units necessary to achieving change, then we should find ways to share the proceeds. If, for example, large savings would accrue to a central purchasing office through a redesigned process, one can agree to share them with the departments willing to participate in the change. On the other hand, if process savings can only be harvested as fractions of full-time staff members across many organizational jurisdictions, then budget savings may not happen at all, short of massive reorganization. We should know when to forgo such savings joyously, acknowledging that good people will find other productive pursuits for their newly found time. This issue is at the heart of our failure to capture the budget savings promised through process redesign.

- *Underpromise and overdeliver*. Never overstate or mislead people's expectations. Be the first to announce new knowledge of project problems. Otherwise, you destroy trust, which is much harder to regain than lose.

- *Consistently learn from your successes and mistakes*. Create and sustain information feedback required to learn. Conduct post mortems at every project milestone.

- *Persist.* Remember that everyone's time is a scarce resource. If you can spend time when all about you are attending to other things, your agenda has a better chance.

- *Create locally adaptive business processes and technology solutions.* Remember that universities are different from those firms that economists or even Cyert and March (1963) described. We are organized anarchies, loosely coupled organizations. Different departments may need to do things differently. Knowing when to hold and when to fold—with respect to those uniform business processes we just know would yield massive economies of scale—is a learnable art. All implementation is local!

There you have it, a baker's dozen plus one of change management maxims and tactics. Readers can assess for themselves whether they are derivable from, or at least consistent with, the literature and the three easy lessons cited above. But if we are to meet the organizational challenge that we are just coming to understand from our change initiatives of the recent past, we must think organizationally. Processes and technology are not enough. People are preeminent.

References

Cohen, M. D., and March, J. G. *Leadership and Ambiguity: The American College President.* New York: McGraw-Hill, 1974.

Cyert, R. M., and March, J. G. *A Behavioral Theory of the Firm,* Englewood Cliffs, N.J.: Prentice Hall, Inc., 1963.

Developing a 21st-Century Workforce for California Government. Report of the Governor's 21st-Century Training Action Team. Sacramento, Calif.: Department of Personnel Administration, 1998.

Hammer, M. "Reengineering Work: Don't Automate, Obliterate." *Harvard Business Review.* July-Aug. 1990.

Hammer, M., and Champy, J. *Reengineering the Corporation: A Manifesto for Business Revolution.* New York: HarperCollins Publishers, Inc., 1993.

Lewin, K. "Preface." In Schein, E. H., *The Corporate Culture Survival Guide*. San Francisco: Jossey-Bass, 1999.

Schein, Edgar H., *The Corporate Culture Survival Guide*. San Francisco: Jossey-Bass, 1999.

Shakespeare, W. *Julius Caesar*, act 4, scene 3, lines 218–219.

Simon, H. A. *Administrative Behavior*. (2nd ed.) New York: Free Press, 1965.

Sustaining Excellence in the 21st Century: A Vision and Strategies for the University of California's Administration. Report and Recommendations of the New Campus Administrative Support and Ancillary Services Planning Group, University of California, Los Angeles, Mar. 1991.

Weick, K. E. *The Social Psychology of Organizing*. (2nd ed.) New York: McGraw-Hill Higher Education, 1979.

Young, C. E. *Transforming Administration at UCLA—A Vision and Strategies for the 21st Century*. Unpublished internal document. Los Angeles: University of California, Sept. 1991.

10

The Policy Challenges

Richard N. Katz and Rhonda I. Gross

The unprecedented flow of information across networks and between organizations, coupled with the power of computer systems to extract, compile, organize, and republish information, has made e-business possible. These same capabilities are also raising significant concerns and issues related to the appropriate use of institutional information and to the protection of information originating or residing in college and university information systems.

The closing chapter of this book accurately describes the developmental phase facing colleges and universities today on the road to enabling e-business as one of *integration*. Our progress in adopting e-business in higher education will be enabled or constrained by institutions' ability to develop, implement, enforce, and automate complex rules that authorize these consumers to partake of university services. For example:

- What rights will distant learners have vis-à-vis access to licensed university information resources?

- How can colleges and universities protect usage logs that record student and faculty library consumption activity for materials licensed from third parties?

Note: The authors wish to thank Gary Gatien of the University of Michigan for his significant research in support of this writing.

- What information can and should development offices acquire and maintain on prospective donors?

The privacy, access, ownership, and security issues posed by e-business are extraordinarily complex and represent as much a set of cultural, behavioral, and policy issues as technical ones.

Colleges and universities have long—and correctly—been described as self-governing anarchies or adhocracies. Higher education's hallowed and well-established traditions of self-governance and shared governance are responsible for our remarkable history of achievement, service, and innovation. These traditions also make integration hard. In many ways, achieving the necessary level of technical integration to enable e-business is the least complex aspect of preparing the institution for e-business. Many campus chief information officers (CIOs) understand what it means to reorient systems from their current functional office views to the end user views (those of students, parents, alumni, and the inter-enterprise) that e-business will demand. In most cases, the technical tools to achieve this kind of integration exist. In short, technical integration is a significant issue that can be addressed by vision, talent, and money. The thornier integration challenges are cultural and relate to role definitions, authority and power, and values. These issues will define the boundaries of an institution's approach to, and its likelihood of success in, implementing e-business.

The Need for a Policy Framework to Support Portals and E-Business

In a far-sighted article, Graves, Jenkins, and Parker (1995) describe the development of an electronic information policy framework. As e-business drives the Internet and the Web from an infrastructure for storing static information to one over which much of the institutional mission is delivered, the need for such a policy framework becomes overwhelming. Although the existence of sound information policies will not guarantee entrée into the world of e-business, the lack of these policies will guarantee nonentrance. Colleges and universities will need to develop a cohesive and consistent set of policies that will guide the members of their communities in a number of areas, including:

- Digital identity and the access to institutional technology and information resources

- Use of the institution's name and trademarks

- Acquisition, retention, and disposition of information resources

- Ownership of information in institutional systems and the management of intellectual property rights

Each of these issues is enormously complex, and colleges and universities worldwide have struggled with them for years. No attempt will be made in this chapter to specify solutions in these areas. Rather, the purpose of this chapter is to relate the necessity of developing a holistic electronic information policy framework to efforts to implement e-business.

Digital Identity and Access to Institutional Technology and Information Resources

One issue of importance is that of digital identity. In the technical context, colleges and universities must develop the means to authenticate an individual as him- or herself, to recognize the individual as a member of the institutional community, and to confer upon or deny this individual different rights and authorities as a community citizen. In physical reality, these activities are transacted in a variety of complex formal or informal ways: we can demand photo ID cards, check signature files, or wave to the familiar librarian who regulates access to the closed stacks. The regulation of access to institutional resources in the physical context is governed by a tapestry of policies, procedures, customs, norms, and historical happenstance that computers are not yet intelligent enough to deal with. Instead, computers depend on precise information that derives absolute answers to the questions (1) Are you who you claim to be? and (2) Are you allowed to . . . (consume this service, enter this building, use this parking lot)?

Not only is this a technical challenge of enormous proportions, it is also a policy quagmire requiring colleges and universities to make explicit and public distinctions about the rights and privileges that accrue to different members of the academy. What rights does the president's spouse really have? What rights do lecturers have, relative to career-ladder faculty? These policy issues will get more complex as colleges and universities move into distance education and implement "cradle-to-endowment" strategies to create relationships with promising applicants, lifelong learners, and potential donors.

Of course, it is important to note that for public institutions, managing access to institutional information must be situated in the context of public records laws, which, themselves, are hard to reduce to simple rules that can be automated.

Use of the Institution's Name and Trademarks

The Internet and the World Wide Web are, among other things, a publishing infrastructure. Web technology is relatively simple to program as well as to use, allowing "a thousand flowers to bloom." At nearly every college and university, myriad operational and dead Web pages make volumes of campus information and misinformation available to anyone with an Internet connection.

Many institutions today provide incoming students with sufficient disk storage to encourage their development of personal Web sites. Of course, into every flower garden will come the occasional weed, snail, or predator. From a policy perspective, the challenge posed by the Internet and the Web is the challenge of cultural integration. Colleges and universities must specify policies that regulate the appropriate use of these very public resources. This is an extra-ordinarily complex area to govern. At stake are a variety of dire legal and public relations issues. These issues can include

- Pornographic materials on official institutional sites

- Sale of advertising on pages containing campus trademarks

- Creation of fraudulent sites

- Commercial use of campus resources for personal gain

- Trademark infringement

- E-harassment and other activities that create a hostile e-environment

- Neglect of sites that make inaccurate, anachronistic, and obsolete information available to legislators, trustees, donors, auditors, and others

All of these issues can and will emerge within the broader policy contexts that typically respect and encourage free expression by members of the institution's community. As Graves, Jenkins, and Parker advise, "any policy will need to balance the institution's role in protecting access to sensitive or potentially objectionable information and its role in supporting an individual's right of free expression" (1995, p. 18). This difficult balancing act is hardly new, but it is complicated by the levels of integration anticipated by e-business applications.

Acquisition, Retention, and Disposition of Information Resources

E-business, in much of the popular literature, begins with something called "e-tailing," the marketing of the enterprise to its existing or prospective clients. In one context, for example, higher education institutions have been doing this for years. Each year, colleges and universities acquire the files of high school students who achieve high scores on the PSAT and shower these college-bound tenth and eleventh graders with literature extolling the virtues of their campuses. In an e-business context, smart and aggressive institutions will acquire more and more information in the competition for the "best" students. These institutions will likely develop robust profiles of students to match against the target profiles of successful applicants. Similarly, the pathologies of university hospital patients will be profiled for matching against promising experimental drugs and therapies for possible "targeting" of such patients for clinical trials.

These practices are entrepreneurial, effective (relative to their goals), and probably beneficial, as college-bound students "want" to be discovered and patients want access to the best modes of treatment available. However, the unprecedented ability of institutions to acquire personal information, to combine this information in unique ways, and to store massive amounts of this information on individuals who may (or may not) be part of the institutional community, will raise significant privacy and security issues in the future. New policies regarding what kind of information is to be collected, how it is to be used, and for how long it is to be retained, will become increasingly important. The failure to develop new standards of practice in this area will invite new regulation of this area of institutional activity. The issue of individual and institutional access to this kind of information will also rise in importance and must be dealt with explicitly in campus information policy.

In addition to developing the technologies and policies to ensure privacy and to secure and protect information under institutional management, colleges and universities will need to devise and implement new policies to describe, manage, and protect related classes of information. Such classes of information include confidential information (tenure and promotion files), proprietary information (patent, trademarks, copyrights), privileged information (attorney-client communications, counseling files), and trade information (public-private research activities). E-business, among other things, assumes an unprecedented level of interoperation among the systems and data resources of "trading partners." In the future, campus suppliers will have access to institutional procurement systems, as will publishers, high schools, consortium partners, and others. This integration of systems and information will demand that policies and contracts regulate the acquisition, use, retention, and disposition of information by others in the newly extending community. This has already become a very complex area of policy development at research universities where the university values of open sharing of research findings clashes with desires of private clinical research sponsors to protect information as proprietary.

A final area of concern under this broad umbrella is the management of licensed software and information resources. Campus information policy must respect the rights of authors and distributors. Evolving technologies and law will likely enhance authors' and distributors' ability to track the use of their licensed property and perhaps even to implement campuswide penalties when infringements are identified.

Ownership of Information and Intellectual Property Rights

Information policy must seek to distinguish the ownership status of information embodied in institutionally owned digital storage and transport media from the responsibilities for managing this information. Information policies should strive to define the standards and care with which information resources must be managed, while recognizing the inherently decentralizing tendencies of networked information and resources. Most information policy frameworks that address networked information define and articulate a concept of information stewardship that allows the Web of campus-related information to evolve in a fashion that balances the needs of individuals and local campus units with those of the institution as a whole.

Perhaps the most complex aspect of preparing the campus information policy environment for e-business is the set of policy issues surrounding the ownership and management of intellectual property generated on the campus. Whereas colleges and universities have developed robust policies for the ownership and management of intellectual property protected by patents, the rights to intellectual property developed by faculty members and protected by copyright have traditionally remained with individual faculty members. To be frank, the total economic value of published college and university intellectual property has been small historically, and the institutional investment in the creation of this property has also been small.

The application of Internet, Web, and other information technologies to the core educational mission of higher education is changing all of this. Today, pioneering faculty members are investing considerable time and energy to Web-enable their courses. Institutions, in many cases, are partnering with these faculty members by providing grants to purchase release time from other obligations and by placing a variety of technical tools at the faculty member's disposal. For the first time, course materials organized in this fashion can reach beyond the confines of the classroom, hence changing simultaneously the cost structure, the investment model, and the economic value of traditional course materials. Courses created in this fashion become courseware and begin to accrue many of the attributes of books, which also are evolving to become more interactive.

As the e-learning aspect of the e-business revolution evolves, institutions, their faculty members, and publishers are looking at faculty course materials as scalable economic goods that can be modularized. New pedagogical standards are evolving, in concert with new neuroscientific findings about the learning process. Institutions such as the University of Phoenix and Great Britain's Open University are investing millions in curricula for networked delivery. Faculty course notes on the Web are being reportedly pirated and repackaged for distribution by new proprietary e-business enterprises. In sum, the new potential posed by the integrated technologies of e-business suggest the need for new policies regarding the ownership and management of rights to faculty course materials.

Framed creatively, this discussion and faculty and institutional investments can draw new students into the campus community and, in some cases, bring new revenue to the institution. Such changes are, however, countercultural and could also lead to new divisions on the campus. As noted in Chapter Six, e-business is likely to change the way institutions operate. It is a mission-critical undertaking that will challenge long-standing institutional policies and will therefore demand the careful application of change management techniques and processes.

Elements of an Integrated Policy Framework

Although each institution will develop a policy that best reflects its priorities, strategies, values, and history, a policy framework should contain certain elements. The list that follows is offered as a starting point to encourage the reader to begin.

Critical Assumptions

The institution will balance the rights of individuals with the institution's responsibility to make information available to support the mission. The role of the central campus is to articulate the standards of data access and integrity and to differentiate user rights and privileges so as to achieve such a balance. A key question that will need to be considered is, under what conditions (responsibilities of resource users) and for what members of the community are access to the network, network-based services, and networked information a basic right of the campus community?

Operating Principles

Policies are, by definition, value-laden. Institutions can be well served by considering bounding the framework by principles. At many institutions (particularly public), information policy is bounded by principles that

- Identify the responsibility for making information available

- Limit the institution's regulatory responsibility for information for which it is not responsible

- Assume institutional responsibility for defining access privileges to its information for classes of users

Such a policy framework and those of other leading institutions also outline in broad terms a variety of legal, ethical, technical, governance, and economic issues for the purpose of acculturating the policy reader to the complexity of the issues and to the basic values of the institution.

Information Access and Security

It will be important to establish the notion that institutional electronic information resources—including data, applications, systems, hardware, software, and networks—are valuable. Institutional assets, including electronic information resources, must be protected according to the nature of the risk and to the sensitivity and criticality of the resource being protected. Information policy should endeavor to identify major classes of information assets requiring protection and assign to them differential levels of protection. Information classes might include privileged information, personal information, personnel information, public records, and so forth.

Areas in which security-related policies need to be addressed include the following, drawn from the University of California's *Business and Finance Bulletin IS-3* (Nov. 1998):

- *Logical security.* The policy should identify security measures to be enforced through software, network, or procedural controls (such as version management) as well as communications security and reduction of risk from intrusive computer software. Various measures include end-user access controls, system administration access controls, applications software development and change control, and controls on data backup, retention, data privacy, and data transfers and downloads. Encryption policies will also need to be developed, as these capabilities become ubiquitous, as will policies that specify which applications and resources must be protected by firewalls.

- *Physical security.* Even in an e-business environment, there are physical disaster controls and access controls (for example, for check stock and other financial instruments) that must be covered by institutional policy.

- *Managerial security.* Although there are unique risks inherent in the management of electronic and, particularly, networked information resources, many of the risks remain people-related. An information policy framework should attempt to integrate institutional policy related to bonding and background checking for personnel with access to sensitive and critical information. Procedures to implement such policies should also identify the processes for altering authorities when changes in duties or employment status occur.

- *Responsibilities.* An information policy framework must identify both those responsible for maintaining the policy and those responsible for its implementation. Ideally, policy compliance escalation procedures should be specified.

- *Definitions and authorities.* A policy framework should define key terms such as *authorized user, disaster, security, virus,* and others. Information management roles such as stewardship and proprietorship should also be defined. Regulations and laws that govern an institution's access and security policies should be referenced, including public records law.

- *Digital certificates*. An emerging technology to meet the needs of electronic security in the networked context is the use of public key infrastructure and digital certificates. This technology is being developed to address authorization and authentication. Institutions that implement certificate authorities and digital certificates will need also to develop congruent policies that identify processes for approving authorities, standards for certificates, and identification of certificates. Policies will also have to be enacted to govern whether certificates are issued to individuals, servers, or certificate authorities, what the responsibilities of these authorities are, and what the expiry dates of these certificates will be. Finally, policy in this evolving arena will need to describe the processes for registering and issuing certificates, for maintaining a repository of certificates and public keys, for revoking or renewing certificates, and for managing the certificate authority's private key.

Disaster Protection and Business Continuity

Institutions must also develop policy environments that protect their information resources systems and services.

- The information policy framework should describe the institution's plans, policies, and procedures for assuring business continuity, including plans for testing critical systems periodically.

- The disaster recovery plan should identify emergency response procedures, and it should specify teams of personnel responsible for responding to emergency situations.

E-mail

Although e-mail is not specifically a tool of e-business, its governance as a critical element of the overall campus information policy framework is crucial. Institutions are advised to develop specific policies related to electronic mail that establish the following:

- E-mail accounts as institutional property

- The institution's service commitments regarding e-mail

- The ownership of information produced and received using e-mail accounts

- Institutional access to information in mail accounts under normal or extraordinary (emergency or investigative) conditions

- Allowable use, including use for individual commercial gain, representations, and false identity

- Security and confidentiality of information in e-mail accounts

- Individual and institutional responsibilities and authorities for ensuring compliance with policy

Intellectual Property

Policy related to the management and ownership of intellectual property is most complex. For intellectual property not developed on campus and covered by copyrights, patents, licenses, or other contracts, the policy parameters tend to be straightforward.

- Software residing on institutional hardware must be used according to the terms specified under the appropriate software license agreement.

- The institution is responsible for compliance with licenses entered into by the institution on behalf of members of its community. The institution should maintain the right to revoke licensed privileges in cases where violations have been identified. Substantial violations of license conditions should be specified under policy, as should the process for investigating alleged misuse and for implementing remedial action.

- Information resources, such as databases, books, journal articles, and the like, are governed by either copyright law or license agreements with their publishers. Institutional policy should affirm the rights of authors, publishers, and distributors to their intellectual property, it should define what constitutes "fair use" in the context of law and licenses, and it should identify the processes for investigating alleged misuse and for implementing remedial action.

- For intellectual property developed on campus, the institution must distinguish between so-called works-for-hire and other works produced in the discharge of an employee's work-related role(s).

- The ownership of a work-for-hire is generally assumed to be the property of the institution. The information policy framework should make explicit reference to the institution's assumptions about what works are considered to be works-for-hire and what ownership rights the institution wishes to assert. This policy should also specify what rights individuals creating works-for-hire may have (publication of a work report in a professional journal), and what the process is for securing individual access to such works.

- The rules of policies related to ownership of other intellectual property produced by members of the campus community are more likely to be specified in an institution's faculty handbook, or in policy covering patents, or even in policy covering conflict of interest and commitment (Thompson, 1999). As the boundaries between course materials and published materials begin to blur, institutions will need to revisit the ownership issues as part of an integrated information policy framework.

Policy is, by its nature, soft, squishy, and difficult. As previously mentioned, policy development and the policy environment are inherently value-laden, and therefore there are no cookbooks or detailed instructions for their formulation. Policies are for the most part context-specific. A bible college's definition of appropriate use of technology will likely differ from that of a public research university.

Policy can be integrative, and integration is the mandate that looms ahead for institutions seeking to implement e-business solutions. Colleges and universities anticipating the move to e-business must recall that e-business, in many areas, is not merely the application of new technology to old processes. E-business applications will open new vistas and create new risks. Extending the name and reach of your college or university can and will swell the ranks of members of your communities. As e-communities grow, opportunities grow. Along with opportunities, fraud, abuse, and misuse will also grow. An integrated information policy framework will be hard to institute. On the other hand, an integrated, e-business environment without a supporting policy framework will be nearly impossible to manage.

References

Graves, W., Jenkins, C., and Parker, A. "Development of an Electronic Information Policy Framework." *CAUSE/EFFECT*, Summer 1995, pp. 15–23. [http://www.educause.edu/ir/library/pdf/cem9524.pdf].

Thompson, D. "Intellectual Property Meets Information Technology." *Educom Review*, 1999, 34(2), 14–21. [http://www.educause.edu/ir/library/html/erm99022.html].

University of California. *Business and Finance Bulletin IS-3: Electronic Information Security*, Nov. 1998. [http://www.ucop.edu/ucophome/policies/bfb/is3.pdf].

11

Summing Up

Richard N. Katz and Larry Goldstein

This volume began with Richard Katz's effort to untangle the concept and the rhetoric around portal technologies. When introduced, the concept of portals was seized by marketers as information technology's "next big thing" and soon became laden with meanings and expectations beyond its potential. In higher education, business officers, development officers, and campus presidents enthusiastically envisioned new forms of customer care and, more importantly, new revenue sources, while faculty cried foul at the prospect of seeing commercial advertising creep into the campus Web space. Information technologists on campus organized around portals in the fashion of a search for the Holy Grail, believing portals could solve vexing content management, navigation, and information security issues.

In the two or three years since their introduction, portals have been put into context. In the institutional context, portals are indeed an important technical and visual superstructure for organizing online resources and services. Portals are considered to be a critical layer of so-called middleware that enables users of the institutional Web to customize, personalize, and tailor resources and services in ways that fit the users' needs and preferences. From a business perspective, the portal and associated technologies are key elements of a new business architecture that includes e-business, online transaction services, customer relationship management, and other capabilities. Portals are neither a technological silver bullet, nor a source of untold riches, nor just another shiny new toy. Portals have the potential to change how an institution appears to its primary stakeholders, but change, as always, comes at a price. This volume is concerned as much with the institutional impacts of portals as the technology of portals.

Portals and e-business are transformational concepts that, for many, are keyed to technological advances. Although there is a great deal of truth in this statement, it is also true that the technology needed to accomplish transformational purposes is only one part of what is necessary to create robust e-business environments in higher education.

What emerges from the organization of this volume is a conclusion that e-business is not merely application of technology to existing business processes. Instead, e-business is helping to create entirely new business practices, in addition to enhancing existing ones. With the capabilities created through the introduction of so-called infomediaries, the integration of portals with the campus Web, e-services, Internet security, enterprise resource management (ERP), and customer relationship management (CRM) capabilities represents a significantly new opportunity area for higher education.

New Business Opportunities

Higher education institutions have been forced to make significant shifts in their business strategies in response to the increased expectations of their constituencies. For example, Oblinger and Goldstein (in Chapter Six) detail changed expectations relating to instantaneous responsiveness, operating efficiencies, and overall cost containment achieved through e-business. The net impact of these rising expectations is an increased emphasis on operating effectiveness. Despite sometimes high initial investments, e-business is moving colleges and universities toward self- and full-service models that eliminate unneeded human intervention in transactional activities.

This has the dual advantage of being able to meet customers' needs whenever they arise—routinely in 24x7 mode—and freeing up staff resources to engage in higher value activities.

Service Delivery

At the core of e-business for colleges and universities is the reexamination of how new technologies can enable the transformation of service delivery. In Chapter Two, Lightfoot and Ihrig describe the University of Washington's approach to providing information when it is needed, where it is needed, and in a format supportive of action. Using service as the driving force, they have redefined customers and placed them at the center of the university's service delivery model. The power of this approach is especially significant in light of the university's decision to continue its reliance on its legacy systems. In essence, the institution remains competitive by extending the life of the existing transaction systems while still moving forward to deliver information needed by its constituents. The beneficiaries are the students, prospective students, patients, donors, and supporters of the athletic programs, as well as the university's myriad other constituents.

The concept of service is completely redefined when one considers the thirteen million hits received monthly by the University of Minnesota's student Web site. Kvavik suggests (in Chapter Five) the awesome effort it would take to replicate manually the three million pages of information being downloaded from the site on a monthly basis and points out that the shift in service delivery is only the beginning of the transformation expected in response to the new technology. When e-business concepts are fully deployed to teaching and learning, new value will be discovered within the educational process.

The focus of enterprise resource planning systems represents a comprehensive approach to data consolidation, enabling institutions to examine their full range of activities in a holistic manner.

E-business takes this several steps further by shifting the focus from processes to information. And possibly of greatest significance is the emphasis on allowing customers to determine the information and services they will access through the use of portals.

Stakeholder Relationship Management

Colleges and universities have sought lifetime relationships with students since the establishment of the first alumni association, if not before. Campuses seek to maintain connections with alumni for several reasons, not the least of which is the role alumni play in perpetuating our institutions through their philanthropic activities. With today's technology, these lifetime relationships take on an entirely new meaning. The concept of "cradle-to-endowment" relationships remains an important one, but other connections take on new significance as well. The idea that a prospective student can establish a lifetime relationship based on an initial visit to an institution's Web site has become a reality for many colleges.

This is symbolic of the customer relationship management shift described by Grant and Anderson in Chapter Three. Customer or stakeholder relation management is the next step in the evolution begun during the 1990s, when ERPs focused on reengineering operating processes to reduce costs and improve efficiencies. In today's environment, institutions are placing students, prospects, parents, patients, and alumni at the core of their educational and business strategy. Thinking of stakeholders in this way is consistent with the more global evolution of higher education from a producer-centered industry to one that is consumer-centered. Higher education is ideally positioned to learn from the successes of other industries that have experienced this shift—primarily those in the commercial sector. Although only a portion of what has occurred in the commercial sector will have relevance for higher education, much can be learned from the examination of their success and failure.

Portals

One area in which much can be learned from the commercial sector is that of portals. Strauss (in Chapter Four) describes two types of portals: horizontal enterprise portals (HEPs), or megaportals, and vertical enterprise portals (VEPs). Colleges and universities are learning from the successes of HEPs, such as Yahoo! and Netscape, but the most successful portal solutions for campuses will inevitably be VEPs. The portal defined by Strauss is a "single CPAD—a customized, personalized, adaptive desktop." He goes on to describe an environment wherein each user will use a unique portal, reflecting his or her role, needs, and interests. Relying on a single sign-on accomplishing both authentication and authorization, individual users will have access to information and functionality based on their preferences and needs.

Technology Implications

Although we have suggested that the technology is only one factor in the evolution of e-business for higher education, it should not be assumed that the technology is without its complications. The specific technology decisions required today are incredibly important, and if they are not planned appropriately, they will represent significant costs. These costs may take the form of wasted expenditures due to abandoned investments, or, more likely, they will appear in the form of opportunity costs. Katz and Gross (in Chapter Ten) remind us that technology planning in higher education environments is complicated and confounded by the juxtaposition of complex and highly distributed decision styles and norms with fast-moving technologies.

Daigle and Cuocco (in Chapter Eight) and Gleason (in Chapter Seven) address aspects of this situation from the perspective of a large public comprehensive university and a private, selective college, respectively. Each identifies and explores the range of technical opportunities surrounding portal technologies and outlines how institutional priorities influence weights and choices among alternative platforms. Their experiences reinforce the idea that no specific approach is right for every institution. Technology decisions and priorities, in the final analysis, are guided and reinforced by the cultural and technical contexts in which they must be implemented. The California State University and Boston College examples illuminate the thought and action processes that institutions must go through to acculturate technologies that are likely to become pervasively used by members of the institutional community. Their experiences can help position other institutions to take advantage of the e-business opportunities present in today's environment without prescribing specific solutions. Without such a plan—incorporating input from diverse campus sectors, including information technology, the business office, academic affairs, development, and athletics—institutions will likely be positioned poorly to respond to these e-business opportunities. Given the uncertainties and changes in the vendor community that drive much of e-business activity, it becomes even more critical that institutions be prepared to make the decisions that are best for them.

Policies

The most difficult aspect of e-business for many colleges and universities will be the development of the institutional policies required to support it. As Katz and Gross point out in Chapter Ten, "the privacy, access, ownership, and security issues posed by e-business are extraordinarily complex and represent as much a set of cultural, behavioral, and policy issues as technical ones." Although Gleason (Chapter Seven) is able to summarize in a useful list the steps that need attention to establish the technology needed to support e-business at one university, no such list exists for the policy decisions required to leverage, support, monitor, or control the e-business opportunities facing campuses today. Each situation will be different. For some campuses, attention will center on the reputation of the institution and the appropriateness of introducing advertising to the institution's Web pages. For others, the focal point will be ownership of intellectual property. For others, the critical issue will be the identification of the appropriate institutional officer to make decisions about which business opportunities will be pursued and which ones will not be considered. Each of these issues has the potential to stimulate heated debate within the academy. The debate needs to begin immediately because the opportunities are here today.

People

In Chapter Nine, Curry reminds us that the success of any technology-enabled change initiative ultimately rests on the ability of leaders to inspire change and of people to embrace change. Curry presents the view that experience *and* the new technologies suggest the need to transform the manner in which transformation is crafted and communicated in higher education. The new technologies will indeed transform our institutions but will do so through the management of a steady stream of service innovations that are delivered in an integrated fashion through the institutional portal. In this way, change is likely to be perceived as being gradual, and in general it will be associated with service enhancements, thereby lowering the oft-experienced resistance to change. Portal and related technologies make it possible to rethink the confederated relations between the campus central administrative organizations and the organizational subunits of the institution. Such a rethinking is enabled by standards enforced by the portal—standards that empower solutions wherever they may emerge so long as these solutions belong to the institution and conform in certain critical ways to institutional standards.

Conclusion

The Internet has held the promise of financial value ever since its inception. Only now are colleges and universities truly recognizing the magnitude of its potential. The irrational boom and bust of the so-called New Economy suggest to us that caution and enthusiasm are both warranted. Emerging technologies are making clear both a new business architecture[1] and a new technical architecture to foster higher education's mission. These architectures put a design accent on modularity, flexibility, and nimbleness and are focused on presenting institutional services and information in ways that conform to the needs of stakeholders rather than the needs of unaligned functional organizations. This potential is enormously powerful and, in fact, it may be quietly revolutionary. Once information that previously resided in stovepiped organizations can be brought to the surface and joined with information from other organizations, students, faculty members, staff members, parents, and others can make new inferences about the institution and can begin to reorient the behaviors of the institution. Once our technologies make it possible to facilitate the building of a relationship with a prospect or a patient and to follow such individuals throughout their decades of involvement with our institutions, new relationships can be enabled.

The technologies of portals, e-business, customer relationship management, and so forth, are making it possible for us to create compelling virtual environments to accompany our compelling campus environments. Bricks and clicks. It is clear that our great institutions will not only survive this new wave of technology, they will also embrace it in ways that foster higher education's purpose. In fact, we hope that these technologies will extend higher education's purpose across distance and time in ways that knit our institutions even more deeply into the very fabric of our stakeholders' lives.

Note

1. See "UC2010: A New Business Architecture for the University of California," http://uc2010.ucsd.edu (University of California: July 2000).

Readings

Aldrich, C. "Learning Portals and the E-Learning Hype Cycle." Gartner Group Research Note, Mar. 3, 2000.

Barnick, D., Smith, D., and Phifer, G. "Q and A: Trends in Internet and Enterprise Portals." Gartner Group Research Note, Sept. 27, 1999.

Blumenstyk, G. "Colleges Get Free Web Pages, But With a Catch: Advertising." *Chronicle of Higher Education*, Sept. 3, 1999.

Connolly, C. "From Static Web Site to Portal." *EDUCAUSE Quarterly*, 2000, *23*(2), 38–41.

Ethridge, R., and others. "Building a Personalized Education Portal." *EDUCAUSE Quarterly*, 2000, *23*(3), 12–19.

Fenn, J., and Linden, A. "2000 Hype Cycle of Emerging Technologies." *Gartner Group Monthly Research Review*, July 1, 2000, pp. 1–2.

Harris, K., and others. "Important Distinctions Between Enterprise Portals and Knowledge Management." *InSide Gartner Group*, Aug. 25, 1999.

Harris, K., and others. "The Enterprise Portal: Is It Knowledge Management?" Gartner Group Research Note, Aug. 2, 1999.

Harris, M., and Yanosky, R. "Higher Education Enterprise Portals." Gartner Group Research Note, May 2, 2000.

"Higher Education Portals." IBM Global Education Industry White Paper.

KPMG Consulting, "Portal White Paper." Oct. 2000.

Looney, M., and Lyman, P. "Portals in Higher Education." *EDUCAUSE Review*, 2000, *35*(4), 28–37.

Olsen, F. "Colleges Collaborate on Software That Would Allow Ad-Free 'Portal' Sites." *Chronicle of Higher Education*, June 9, 2000.

"Online Community Portals." *Multiversity*, Fall 2000.

Phifer, G. "CIO Alert: Be Prepared to Support Multiple Portals in Your Enterprise." Gartner Group Research Note, Apr. 19, 2000.

Phifer, G. "Best Practices in Deploying Enterprise Portals." Gartner Group Research Note, July 24, 2000.

Phifer, G. "CIO Update: Major Software Vendors Advance Into Enterprise Portals." Gartner Group Research Note, May 31, 2000.

Phifer, G. "Enterprise Portals: Growing Up Quickly." Gartner Symposium Itexpo 2000, Walt Disney World, Orlando, Fla., Oct. 16–20, 2000.

Phifer, G. "Multiple Portals in Your Enterprise: Count On It." *Gartner Group Monthly Research Review*, May 1, 2000, pp. 1–2.

Phifer, G. "Thirteen Key Partnerships for Enterprise Portal Vendors." Gartner Group Research Note, Mar. 28, 2000.

Sistek-Chandler, Cynthia. "Portals: Creating Lifelong Campus Citizens." *Converge Magazine Supplement*, Oct. 2000.

Smith, D. "A Plague on Portals." Gartner Group Research Note, July 13, 1999.

Strauss, H. "Web Portals: A Home Page Doth Not a Portal Make." *Edutech Report*, 2000, *15*(11).

Yanosky, R. "JA-SIG's Community-Sourced Portal for Higher Education." Gartner Group Research Note, Sept. 5, 2000.

Young, J. "Colleges Create On-Line Education Portal." *Chronicle of Higher Education*, June 25, 1999.

Zastrocky, M., and Phifer, G. "Best Practices in Deploying Institution-Wide Portals." Gartner Group Research Note, Aug. 10, 2000.

Index